Marks of Excellence

Adulting Life Skills Wisdom, Chiseled for Teens to Survive the Modern World

Claire Leeson

Contents

Free Life Skills Print Outs

As a way of saying thanks for your purchase, I'm offering a set of FREE life skills related print-outs to my readers. You will also receive:

- New free bonuses when they are released.
- My future books to read for free before they are published.
- Periodic discounts on my books.

To get instant access, you can **scan the QR code** or go to:

https://podathoughts.com/free-bonus

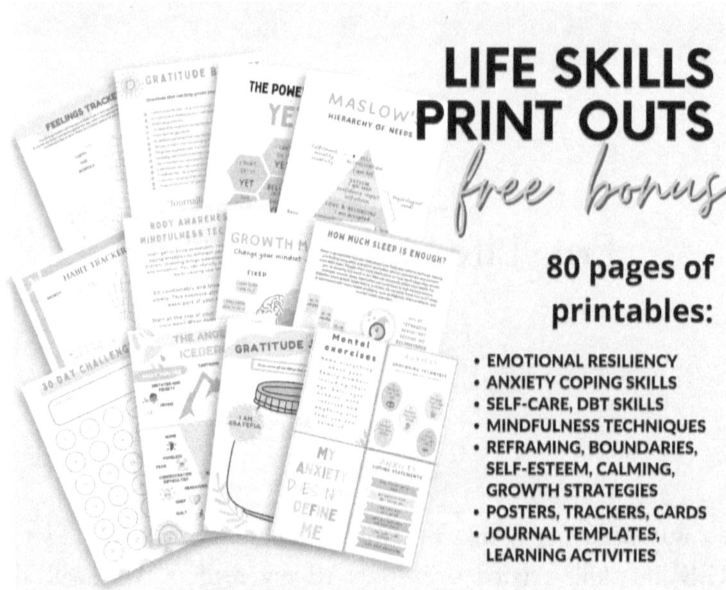

LIFE SKILLS
PRINT OUTS
free bonus
80 pages of printables:
• EMOTIONAL RESILIENCY
• ANXIETY COPING SKILLS
• SELF-CARE, DBT SKILLS
• MINDFULNESS TECHNIQUES
• REFRAMING, BOUNDARIES, SELF-ESTEEM, CALMING, GROWTH STRATEGIES
• POSTERS, TRACKERS, CARDS
• JOURNAL TEMPLATES, LEARNING ACTIVITIES

Introduction

I remember the first time my eldest son, Ethan, visited our family after going away to college. I missed him, and at the same time, I felt so proud of him for becoming such a responsible, independent young man! While we were having lunch together—my husband, myself, and Ethan's two younger siblings—he proudly told us how he had applied for a loan to buy his first car. He also made us laugh with stories about living with his roommate, who couldn't even change a light bulb. Finally, he asked his father for advice as he was having a job interview the following week. My youngest daughter, Sophia, who was 12 by then, exclaimed: "So how come they don't teach us all of this stuff at school?" Ethan shrugged. Then, my three kids turned to me for some reason. Guess what? I didn't know how to answer her either.

It's not easy becoming an adult. And it's not something we achieve overnight or in a big breakthrough. Acquiring all the necessary skills to thrive out there, when you no longer live with your parents and life is something you have to create as you go, takes a lot of time, effort, and trial. Think about it as sculpting: The teen is the already beautiful piece of marble that, through the distilled wisdom of new adulting skills, gets turned into a gorgeous statue of a good, mature, self-reliant, and wise adult in the digital age.

Life already carves its marks on us, but the result will be even better when you are at the same time the marble statue and the sculptor. If you are still in your teens, this is the perfect time to start learning those adulting skills and set yourself up for success!

What Young Adults Face in Our Times

The thing is that, although my eldest son is happy and well-adjusted in his late teens, too many teenagers find themselves overwhelmed and feeling lost as graduation approaches, and the next step in life seems like a leap into the void. Even young adults in their mid-20s are experiencing what experts call "the quarter-life crisis" (Regan, 2022): Feeling trapped, lost, and uninspired for a period that may last up to a couple of years as you figure out who you are and what you want in life. This is how Madeline, a young writer, describes what happened to her at 24 (Miles, 2022):

I felt like I failed, like I couldn't stick to the one plan I had made. I didn't have a solid mental fitness practice to cushion my fall. I was living without purpose or direction. I felt like I lost all agency in my life—and I wasn't sure where I was going to go next. (para. 5)

Quarter-life crises are common for Millennials, as 86% of them say they are experiencing them (Miles, 2022). Things weren't always this way: Former generations used to get married, choose a career path (and stay in it no matter what), and own a home during their 20s. There wasn't much room for doubt or questioning—but there wasn't much freedom of choice, either! The life of young adults nowadays has little to do with that of their aunts, uncles, or their parents, so if you are a twentysomething today, you shouldn't compare yourself to them: "The endless amount of pressure we put on ourselves because of these comparisons (...) often leads to becoming an unhealthy and unhappy young people" (Santillan, 2020).

Experts agree that adolescence has extended and may last up to 25 years old. Teens don't seem in a rush to engage in adult activities, such as driving, getting a job, or even having sex (Stetka, 2017).

However, putting everything on hold as you have no rush to grow up may mean feeling overwhelmed with sudden, unexpected responsibilities later in life. On the other hand, if you start familiarizing yourself early with adulting life skills, this will give you a better perspective.

Why I Wrote This Book

Being the mom of three very different children, and having known dozens of their friends, have helped me understand the challenges most teens face today. They experience tension all the time! They want to become independent, but their parents protect them at all costs. They want to succeed as young adults, but they find college and joining the workforce overwhelming experiences. They may have loving, supportive families who try to guide them, yet the world in which their parents live is so different than their own.

As a counselor, I've talked to many teens. As a mom, I've done my best to guide my three children with their unique traits, goals, and dreams. And finally, I've decided to compile some of the answers they've found more useful with the hope that these nuggets of wisdom can help many other young people as well. I put in the following chapters as many tips and resources as possible so you can start implementing them right away. If by reading this book you feel empowered and more confident in yourself, I'll consider myself happy!

Why will *you* benefit from learning adulting life skills?

• Because you're a young adult who just graduated and is now entering the workforce.

• Because you find yourself away from home for the first time, as a college student overseas or in another state.

• Because you previously had little to no exposure adulting. Maybe your parents were overprotective, and you didn't need to learn these skills before, but now you suddenly find yourself in a situation where you desperately have to acquire them.

• Because, as a special needs adult, you need additional support and resources to learn or to maintain adulting life skills.

• Or maybe, because you're still a teen, but you feel it's never too early to learn!

It's never too late to acquire adulting skills. If you feel you are doing everything wrong (you aren't, trust me!) or if adult life is overwhelming, you'll feel better after applying some of the tips I'll provide. And, of course, the sooner you learn, the better! Acquiring adulting skills at a young age offers better chances at success, better resilience, additional and more effective coping skills, and improved mental well-being.

Okay, so before we get started, let me tell you that my young daughter Sophia was right: Daily living and independence are not taught in schools.

Luckily, this doesn't mean you can't learn them.

Chapter 1

Taking Care of Your Health—You Only Have One Body

 Health is a crown that the healthy wear, but only the sick can see.

— Imam Shafi'i, renowned Islamic scholar known for his wisdom and teachings on various aspects of life.

I REMEMBER when I was a teen (don't ask me how long ago!), every Friday after school, me and my friends would feast on fast food! I drank tons of sodas, and I could eat three double burgers in a row. My usual breakfast was... well, nothing, and I slept until noon during the weekends. My mom bugged me about my health, but I was just fine! Whenever she dragged me to a check-up, everything looked great.

This is what happens to most teenagers: Your body is okay as it is. If you get sick, you recover quickly. You don't get injured as easily as your parents or grandparents. And no matter what you eat, you feel full of energy. It's simple: You are young!

However, as years pass, your health may start taking its toll on you. I remember by the time I was in my early 20s, just one double cheeseburger left me feeling too full to keep on partying. My blood pressure was suddenly higher than expected, and I had to reduce my ingestion of salt and take up regular exercise. After changing some of my habits, I went back to being healthy, but yes, I had to make some changes.

In this chapter, we'll learn how to look after your health before you begin having any real problems. It's never too early to start building good habits. Don't take your physical well-being for granted, learn how to look after your health!

You Don't Own Your Body; Your Body Is Also You!

My son Lucas, now 17, was just like me when I was his age. We had to beg for him to get some fresh air and put down his computer, he skipped meals without realizing it and slept at random hours. One day, I overheard him talking to his dad: "Why would I care about what may or may not happen when I'm 40? I don't want to be a servant of my body; it should serve me instead!" It got me thinking. As long as we consider our bodies a utility, a piece of machinery that's supposed to take us to places, we don't have a proper reason to keep healthy habits. After all, if your car is working fine, why would you waste time and money taking it to the mechanic?

But things would change if we thought of our bodies not as something we *own* but as something we *are*. And sure, you are way more than just your body: Your mind, your dreams, your spirit, your personality, all of those make you into the unique person you are, but your body is also part of you. What's more important: It's difficult to have a happy, healthy mind inside a sick body. And most serious health problems in adulthood can be prevented by establishing good habits right from the start.

Prevention

When you were a kid, your parents regularly took you to your pediatrician. But now that you are in your late teens or early 20s, there's a 50% chance you don't even have a primary care doctor (Markovitz,

2022). You're young and you're healthy, why would regular checkups be your priority anyway?

The problem is that many chronic conditions start to develop at this time in your life and can be harmful if left untreated—high blood pressure or diabetes are just a few examples. Even more importantly, Some of these conditions display early signals and can be reverted with a change of habits. Doing an annual routine checkup is something you shouldn't postpone. When you see your doctor, make sure you discuss your family history. For example, if you have relatives with heart disease, there's a lot you can do to prevent it in the future.

Although many medical tests aren't necessary until later in life, others are important even in your teens. For example, if you have a cervix, you'll need Pap smears every three years starting from your 20s, and anyone sexually active should check for STIs. If you have any risk factors, the doctor may indicate further blood tests for high cholesterol or diabetes. Doctors may also suggest a few vaccines if your calendar of immunizations isn't complete (Markovitz, 2022).

All of the above is about preventing diseases and health conditions. If you are feeling sick, it's important to go see a doctor as soon as possible. Although a common cold or the flu usually improves with rest, drinking plenty of water and some homemade chicken broth, taking medication without supervision can be dangerous.

What You Can Do With New Tech

Besides health insurance, there are important things any young adult should do regarding their health. I suggest you invest in a smart scale you can keep in your bathroom or under your bed. To make your investment even more worth it, consider how it will reap a higher return on investment (ROI) the more years of data it collects and the more insights you get from it.

These devices cost between $20 and $80, depending on the brand, and not only allow you to watch your weight but also keep track of your body fat percentage, your body mass index (BMI), and other biometrics. They connect to your phone with an app and show you your progress in easy-to-understand graphics. The right smart scale won't only show you a number but will also help you develop a better diet and exercise plan according to your personal needs. Additionally, it can record valuable data for monitoring of long-term trends in muscle mass, weight, and even bone density, giving you a more comprehensive picture of your overall health.

Eating Like a Pro

You must remember when puberty hit: How many times did you rush into the kitchen craving some food? By the time girls are about 10 and boys about 12, their growing spurts make them hungrier than ever! Their bodies need those extra calories to support their growth. By the time you reach your late teens, you no longer need to eat as much or as often, as you are no longer growing. However, your specific needs depend on your sex (girls need 25% fewer calories than boys) and your lifestyle: The more intensely you exercise, the more food you need to sustain yourself (*American Academy of Pediatrics*, 2016).

We define "calories" as the units to express the energy supplied by foods. However, eating enough calories isn't the only important thing to consider in a healthy diet: Adolescents and young adults have specific nutritional requirements to help their bodies properly develop and prevent future complications. In other words, it's not about how *much* you eat but about how *well* you eat. So, while filling up on sodas and chips may seem like the average teenage lifestyle, it's never too early to start learning about the right way to feed yourself and create lifelong healthy eating habits. Let's take a closer look at what an ideal teenage diet should include.

What Is Healthy Food?

A good, healthy diet includes a wide variety of foods to cover every nutritional requirement your body needs to stay fit. Here's what you should be eating regularly.

Macronutrients

These are the body's main energy sources, and that's why your body needs them in large amounts.

- **Carbs:** You find them in starches and sugar, and your body should get about 45–65% of the requested calories from them (Kubala, 2022). Not all carbs are the same: Complex carbohydrates fill you up for longer and supply your body with additional nutrients, while simple carbs are delicious but don't fuel you properly. That's why you should try to include whole grains (such as brown rice, oatmeal, or wheat bread) instead of white flour (such as noodles or pizza) in your diet. You'll also find good carbs in fruits and vegetables, which are also full of minerals and vitamins. Include at least two daily cups of fruit and two and a half cups of vegetables in your diet.

- **Proteins:** You'll find them mostly in animal sources, like lean meat, fish, eggs, dairy products, or chicken. You can also find vegetable protein in beans, tofu, or nuts. They are necessary for building your muscles and growing and should make up around 10–35% of your daily calorie intake, maybe more if you are an athlete. However, if you are anything like the average teen in the US, chances are you're eating twice as much (American Academy of Pediatrics, 2016)!

- **Fiber:** It helps you feel full and also stay regular. You obtain it from fruits, vegetables, beans, and nuts. Include them in a wide range of colors. According to your age and gender, you should take between 22–34 grams a day, according to the Dietary Guidelines of America (Kubala, 2022).

- **Fats:** Your body needs some dietary fats to absorb specific vitamins. At the same time, eating fats in excess is bad for your health, as it raises your cholesterol levels and can lead to obesity—a condition suffered by one out of five U.S. teens (Kelly, 2019). As it happens with carbs, you shouldn't forbid yourself from eating fats but choose the best kind instead. Aim for foods high in monounsaturated fat, the healthiest kind, such as peanut oil and peanut butter, cashews, olives and olive oil, walnuts and walnut oil, and canola oil (American Academy of Pediatrics, 2016). Limit your intake of saturated fats, which are found in meat and dairy products, as well as in packaged or processed food. You can also replace a portion of your saturated fats with heart healthy polyunsaturated fats, which can be found in seed oils (sunflower, corn, soybean, flaxseed oils) and cold-water fatty fish, such as salmon, mackerel, tuna, herring, and sardines.

Micronutrients

These are vitamins and minerals your body needs in small but regular supply. Unfortunately, many teens suffer nutritional deficiencies because their diet is not as varied as it should be. Girls are more likely than boys to suffer from such deficiencies. Let's see the most important micronutrients you need to add to your diet.

• **Calcium:** You need this mineral, especially for your bones and teeth. You get it mainly from milk and dairy products. Take three servings a day of low-fat milk, cheese, or yogurt.

• **Vitamin D:** Your body craves this vitamin for proper immune function. You can find it in foods such as orange juice and whole oranges, tuna, and fat-free or low-fat milk. Its deficiency is common among teenagers in the US, and it's affected by different factors, such as "[being] overweight or [having] obesity, having darker skin color, having a medical condition that impacts vitamin D absorption and utilization, and spending little time outdoors" (Kubala, 2022). If your doctor detects such a deficiency, they will suggest a supplement.

• **Vitamin B9 and B12:** They are essential for blood formation and keeping a healthy brain. You will find B9 in foods such as greens (spinach and lettuce), legumes, citrus, banana, and melon. Vitamin B12 is present mostly in animal products such as milk, eggs, meat, and fish. People who follow a vegan diet must take a vitamin B12 supplement to receive this essential nutrient.

• **Vitamin C:** This micronutrient is vital for healing and cannot be produced by the body, so you must add it to your diet. It's present in fruits and vegetables such as lemons, oranges, grapefruits, kiwis, strawberries, tomatoes, bell peppers, and cruciferous vegetables (broccoli, Brussels sprouts, cabbage, cauliflower).

Things to Limit

As long as you eat a healthy, varied diet and you don't have any health conditions, you can allow yourself the occasional treat, such as an ice cream cone, a serving of fries, or a slice of pizza. Food is not only about nutrients but has a social function as well, and sometimes, it's a part of hanging out with your friends. However, certain foods should be limited in your daily meals and only be considered for sporadic consumption.

• **Sugar:** Consuming it in excess may lead you to a series of health conditions, such as obesity, heart disease, and stress and anxiety: "…It's essential for teens to limit foods and beverages high in added sugar like sugary breakfast cereal, sweetened yogurt, pastries, cookies, candy, soda, energy drinks, sweetened coffee beverages, and ice cream" (Kubala, 2022). If you are 2 years or older, it is best to limit the intake of added sugars to less than 10% of your daily calorie intake. That means, for a 2,000 calories diet, you should consume no more than 200 calories, or about 50 grams or 12 teaspoons of sugar (US Department of Agriculture and US Department of Health and Human Services, 2020).

• **Sodium:** Sodium, which is found in table salt, is a necessary mineral, but people usually eat way more than they realize or even need, as processed foods and junk food are full of it. This is terrible news for your heart and blood pressure because it can cause your heart to have to work harder, leading to an increase in your blood pressure. Always choose whole foods instead of packaged ones, and try to limit your intake to 2,300mg a day (visually, this is equal to one teaspoon of salt a day). If you opt for the occasional fast food meal, choose small portions or healthier options, like a veggie wrap or salad instead of fries or fried chicken (Kelly, 2019).

• **Alcohol:** Drinking puts your health at risk. Not only can it poison you and cause irreversible damage to your brain, but alcohol consumption is also linked to high-risk behavior. As an underage drinker, you are more likely to develop an addiction later in life. Even if you are 21, which is the legal drinking age, if you decide to drink alcohol, it must be a moderate consumption.

What Eating Well Also Means

The foods you put on your plate are important, but there's so much more to consider about having a healthy relationship with food. First of all, beware of the dangerous messages social media sends to you and other teens. If you spend a lot of time scrolling your phone looking at pictures of influencers and celebrities, you are more likely to feel dissatisfied with your body and develop a disorder: "Social media exposes teens to unrealistic body and beauty standards as well as dangerous 'diet advice,' and teens are often tempted to mimic the supposed eating patterns of influencers, models, and celebrities" (Kubala, 2022).

Mass media also sends wrong messages through food advertising. By making specific brands look exciting and appealing, and by pretending "all teens" consume specific products, they manipulate you into making wrong food choices: Advertisements, TV shows, the internet, and social media may affect your food and beverage choices and how you choose to spend your time. Many ads try to get you to consume high-fat foods and sugary drinks (Kelly, 2019).

Finally, remember that eating is not only about receiving nutrients but is a social activity as well. Try not to skip any meals, and seize this moment of the day to spend some time with your family, your friends, or your colleagues.

The Importance of Exercise

Regular physical activity is as important for your health as a healthy diet. You should make exercise a part of your routine, whether by taking PE classes at school, practicing a sport you like, doing chores, or choosing the bike instead of the car for going places. Today, we all spend too much time sitting down staring at a screen, no matter our age. Teens should get about 60 daily minutes of vigorous exercise to stay healthy.

Your workout should include intense physical activity at least three times a week. This can be, for instance, running, jogging, dancing, or biking. The good news is that you don't need all the physical activity to take place at once, so if you break it into 15-minute chunks in your routine, you'll be fine. You can even do physical activity indoors: "Routine chores, like cleaning your room or taking out the trash, may not get your heart rate up the way biking and running do, but they keep you moving" (Kelly, 2019).

If you don't enjoy sports, you can still manage to include physical activity and have a great time. Try replacing some of the hours you spend with your friends watching TV, using social media, or playing video games and take the fun outside. Doing a scavenger hunt, playing volleyball, chasing after your dog in the backyard, playing laser tag with your friends, dancing, or playing a game such as *Pokémon Go* will set you on the run!

By the way, technology can be an ally as well! If you are stuck indoors, try exercising at home with a video from YouTube or choose an active sports game on your video console. And get a smartwatch or a fitness watch to track your progress.

Are You Getting Enough Rest?

Sleeping is a natural need, the same as eating and exercising. Not getting enough rest can cause health complications later in life—sleeping less than six hours a day or more than ten is related to a higher risk of dying from cancer (Weng, 2023)—but it also has negative effects on you as a teenager or a young adult as well. You should understand how sleep works to find out your current needs.

Understanding Your Sleep Cycle

During a night of sleep, you experience different states. Sleep occurs in 90-minute cycles that swing between REM sleep and non-REM sleep (which is light sleep and deep sleep). REM is an acronym for Rapid Eye Movement because, in this stage, your eyes are quickly moving under the eyelids, and your brain displays activity as well. It's also the stage where we dream.

While the majority of the 90 minutes consumed by the first half of the night is deep non-REM sleep, it reverses to be dominated by REM sleep in the second half of the night. Experts refer to this as the architecture of sleep (Walker, 2018).

Each of these stages of sleep offers its benefits; that's why you should aim to get a full night of shut-eye every time.

Benefits of Light/Core Sleep

Just falling asleep for a short while can offer you some precious benefits. That's why taking a power nap of 15–20 minutes can feel so invigorating! (But take note not to nap longer than 30 minutes, or you risk slipping into deep sleep, which will leave you feeling groggier and more fatigued for the next 30 minutes to an hour!)

• Light sleep offers better focus and concentration during the day.

• It accelerates physical recovery, boosts muscle growth and repair, and restocks cellular energy.

Benefits of Deep Sleep

This is the predominant stage in the first half of the night. Here are some of the things it can do for you.

• It refreshes your learning and memory capacities.

• It improves muscle memory and skills memory: For sports players, this can lead to reduced sports injuries.

• It removes the toxic protein buildup (known as amyloid plaques) within the brain that kills brain cells and is associated with Alzheimer's. This means that it can potentially reduce the risk or delay the onset of this disease.

Benefits of REM Sleep (The Dreaming State)

This final stage is vital for your mental health for the following reasons:

• It remembers details of the experiences you just lived during that day and integrates them with existing knowledge.

• It is the only time the stress hormones in the body are turned off in the brain.

• It helps you forget or dissolve the emotional pain in your memories. For example, when it comes to trauma or frightening experiences, you will still remember what happened but you will no longer feel the intense pain or sadness, or at least, less so over time.

What Happens When You Don't Sleep Enough?

Although it may be tempting to cut sleep and spend part of the night chatting with your friends or binge-watching shows, you should be aware that sleep debt can't be repaid. You can't "save for later" an extra hour of sleep: If there is insufficient or no sleep on the first night after learning, the chance to consolidate those memories is lost. To make things even worse, sleeping too late will deny the benefits of deep sleep and increase the risk of Alzheimer's. It also impairs learning. And every part of the night is important. Because of the architecture of sleep, waking too early would deny us of our REM "dreaming" sleep, which will prevent the mind from healing from negative experiences and also will impact creativity and learning.

Most teenagers are chronically sleep-deprived and don't know it. General insufficient sleep will lead to reduced concentration and poor muscle recovery, plus it's related to weight gain and obesity. If you get sick or hurt and you don't rest well, your body takes longer to heal. Sleep deprivation is also related to mental health issues such as depression and anxiety.

Finally, consider that sleep isn't only vital for your body to work properly but for you to manage your emotions as well. Sleep to avoid emotional irrationalities. The well invested sleep would translate into less emotional breakdowns, impulses, tempers, and excessive swings of positive and negative emotions for children, teens, and adults.

How to Get Enough Sleep?

Although teenagers are usually night owls, aim at an earlier sleep time: "Research shows that sleeping between the hours of 8 p.m. and midnight sets you up for the best chance at restorative sleep, no matter what time your alarm is set to" (*How much deep, light, and REM*, 2023).

Not only should you notice how many hours of sleep you get, but how much time you spend on each stage:

• As for light sleep, there's no minimum amount required, but spending too much time in this stage could highlight you're not getting enough of the other ones (taking a bunch of catnaps is not the same as sleeping through the night!).

• A second stage of light sleep is usually called "core sleep," and it tends to occupy half of the time you spend asleep.

• The deep sleep stages are where most of the restorative processes happen, and because they take place during the first half of the night, that's the main reason for going to bed as early as possible. You should aim for about one or two hours of deep sleep.

• The REM stage takes place every 90 minutes, and although it's quite short during the first part of the night, it tends to get longer the more you sleep, up to the point REM stages take about 20–25% of your sleep time at nighttime (*How much deep, light, and REM*, 2023).

Considering we need about seven to eight hours of sleep (and I mean you being *asleep* asleep, not just the time you spend in bed), we need to create an appropriate sleep routine that allows us to fully disconnect and rest. Begin by watching what you eat during the night: Avoid fatty food, caffeine, and alcohol. Create a cozy atmosphere in your room by removing any blue light from screens, opting for darkness instead, and keeping the temperature cool. You can add white noise or quiet music to help you relax, and keep to a sleep routine synchronized with your circadian rhythm. This would mean waking at the start of daylight hours even on weekends!

To make sure you're getting enough and adequate sleep, you can get a smartwatch—such as the Apple Watch—that's fully equipped with sensors to work as a sleep tracker. Many apps are also available for setting reminders and organizing a healthy sleep routine.

Keeping Yourself Safe

When looking after your health, another thing to consider is avoiding unnecessary risks and taking care of yourself. When you were a young kid, your parents were always there to protect you. Now, as a teenager or young adult, you'll find that it's up to you to take basic safety precautions. First of all, you need to develop protective behaviors, which are "life skills to recognize safe and unsafe situations. They are the things we say and do to keep ourselves safe" (ACT Government, 2020). Learn how to recognize the signals in your body that allow you to spot potential dangers and surround yourself with a network of people you trust and can help you feel and be safe, both in person and online.

Basic Safety Measures

Too much exposure to crime news can increase your anxiety levels and make you feel stressed all the time. That's why you shouldn't spend all your awake time watching the news or fearing criminals! However, it's important to stay informed and turn on alerts for your area, the same as adding emergency numbers to speed dial in your phone and learning how to use them. Another useful number is a safe car ride you can call if you need someone to drive you, especially at night. You must use this service if you have had any alcohol to drink or are under the influence of any substances.

When you walk, pay attention to your surroundings and trust your gut. If you notice something is odd (for example, you believe someone is following you), it's always better to be safe than sorry: Get inside a store or a restaurant or blend in with a crowd of people until you can get help.

At home, make sure you know your neighbors and never let strangers inside your building or dorm. Always keep your door locked, even if it's just for a quick jog around the block. And if you are going away on vacation, try to get someone you trust to drop by regularly or install a timer for lights so if there are people watching your house, they think there's always someone inside.

Being Safe Online

When you're online, some dangers are identity theft and sexual extortion. Here are some ways to protect yourself:

• Remember to keep up-to-date antivirus and firewalls to protect your equipment.

• Always use reputable sellers and secure websites for all your online shopping and credit over debit cards.

• Never share with anyone your Social Security number (SSN), and don't include it on check or credit receipts (Brown, 2019).

• In case identity theft happens anyway, the first thing you should do is contact the credit bureaus and make sure they place a fraud alert on your file, close all of your accounts, and file a police report to have proof of the incident.

• Don't post explicit photos of yourself online, on messaging platforms, or to anyone you do not trust intimately. You never know who can access them and later blackmail you. Sadly, this isn't hypothetical, and it recently happened to a boy from Michigan. 17-year-old Jordan ended his life after being blackmailed by two men who posed as a young girl and later requested money for not publishing the nude picture the boy unwillingly sent to them (Ley & Hutchinson, 2023). Jordan's father described that the men had, through Instagram and from "the other side of the planet came into my home while we were sleeping and murdered my son" (Hutchinson, 2023).

Asking for Help

Teenagers are potential targets of sexual abuse, which may include any kind of approach that makes you feel uncomfortable: Touching you, making verbal suggestions, or sending you pictures you're not comfortable with. You can—and should—always talk about these situations with a person you trust; it could be a parent, a teacher, a counselor, or a police officer. Abusers try to manipulate their victims by different tactics such as shaming, threatening, bribing, or trying to persuade them that no one will believe them, and that's why you should remember it's *never* your fault! Talk to the people in your circle: Someone *will* listen and help you.

If you were abused online, whether it's sexual abuse or cyberbullying, talk to someone you feel safe with, directly report the abuser to the website, and block them from ever establishing contact with you again.

Throughout this chapter, we've seen why taking care of your body is the first basic adulting skill any teen should learn as soon as possible. It's never too early to establish good eating, sleeping, exercising, and safety habits!

In the past year, my son Lucas drastically improved some of his ways. He started going to bed and waking up at regular times, having a small yet healthy breakfast, and jogging every other day with a friend from the neighborhood. He told me he still doesn't care about his 40s or 50s, but the motivation for adopting better habits is because he feels he's more effective and thinks with more clarity now. Perhaps that's the most important reason for taking care of your health: Not only for fear of the future but to make the best out of your present as well.

Chapter 2

Home Living—With Others or On Your Own

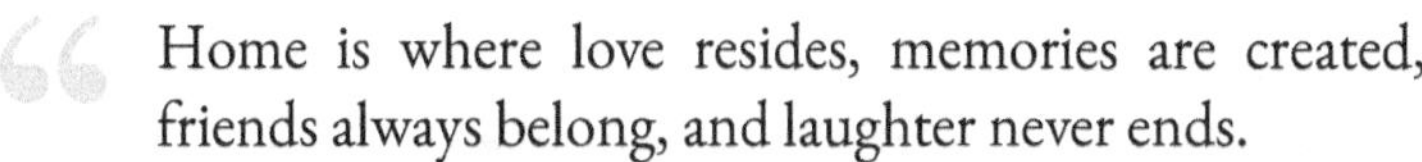

Home is where love resides, memories are created, friends always belong, and laughter never ends.

— Unknown, on what makes a home meaningful and memorable.

MY SON ETHAN moved away from home when he was 18, as he attended college in another state. He felt comfortable in his dorm almost immediately! Being the older son, I think my husband and I expected him to help around more than his siblings, and pretty soon, he learned how to do basic household jobs such as laundry and cooking. With his dad, he learned how to do some minor electrical repairs, and with me, he already knew how to create a weekly menu on a budget. All of this worked out great as he became more independent.

On the other side of the spectrum, I have a teenage daughter, Sophia, who grew up barely doing a thing. In hindsight, I blame myself: She's the youngest and the only girl in the family, and we've all been overprotective of her. It wasn't until she was in middle school that we started requesting something as simple as filling in the dishwasher from her, and still, most of the time, one of her brothers would do the job instead.

In the past year, I've focused on working alongside Sophia to teach her the lesson before it's too late: Mom and Dad won't always be around, so she needs to learn the basics of how to live independently, especially if she wants to follow her big brother's steps and go to college in a few years. If this is your situation as well, or if you're already trying to live away from your family, this chapter will teach you the basics on how to find a proper place, how to get along with others, tips for cooking for one, how to do basic household tasks, and managing small repairs.

Finding a Place to Live

Older teens who move away from their parents because they are attending college have different options. You can either rent an apartment or go live in a dorm together with other students. Let's evaluate their pros and cons, assuming you have a choice: It may all depend on your family's budget and yours, your college's requests (as some of them require freshmen to live in dorms or with a nearby relative), and whatever accommodation you happen to find available at a certain time.

Pros and Cons of Living in a Dorm

Dorms are multi-residential buildings placed on college property and divided into several rooms that usually house one or two students. These buildings being located within the college makes them very convenient for being on time to class! When you pay for your dorm, services usually include Wi-Fi, electricity, and utilities. Some packages include meal plans as well. Besides the bedrooms, dorms have shared spaces such as a kitchen, and sometimes the bathroom is shared as well.

The room you get is pretty small and features no divisions between your stuff and your roommate's. You may even have to share a closet. Some dorms offer further accommodations, such as a sink or a microwave. And here's a possible con: With dorms, you don't get to choose your roommate. This means you share whatever little space you have with someone you may not know at all! Definitely, the lack of privacy is a major drawback for some students. Of course, solid friendships can start in college dorms, and for some students, a dorm helps you seize the "true college" experience and engage in a more active social life after class.

An advantage of dorms is that you don't have to do many chores, as most times, all you need to do is keep your room clean, and that's it! You don't need to pay bills, as your room and board package includes expenses, and besides, since you usually pay for your dorm for a semester, you don't need to pay during the summer if you plan to go back home and stay with your family for a couple of months.

Finally, the process of getting a dorm is way simpler than all the paperwork required for renting an apartment. The sign-up process is pretty straightforward and depends on each school. Besides, you can use the money from your student loan or other financial aid for dorms, but not always for an apartment—we'll get to the topic of rent later in this chapter.

Pros and Cons of Renting an Apartment

Unlike dorms, apartments don't belong to the college but to an individual landlord or a property management company. Therefore, you won't find them as accessible as the typical dorm, and you may need to consider commuting to class. Apartments offer a larger space: Not only do you have a room for yourself, but you also have a private kitchen and bathroom, and some apartment buildings have amenities such as laundry, a swimming pool, or a gym.

Depending on the specific contract, you may be required to pay for the services you use. You'll need to remember to be up-to-date with all your bills and become more responsible. And speaking of payment, although the average rent for an apartment is cheaper than a dorm, you should consider that apartments come with leases, which means there is a contract legally forcing you to pay for a specific period that can be six months or a year. If you go on vacation, you may not opt out of paying rent without risking a penalty.

However, that lack of flexibility can be compensated if you think about the many advantages of living in an apartment: First, you can share the rent with other students, but unlike in dorms, you get to choose your roommates. Second, although you have to respect some basic ground rules, they are way less strict than in dorms, meaning you can arrive at whatever time you want or have visitors over.

Overall, privacy and independence are the main reasons why some students opt out of a dorm and prefer an apartment. Sure, you'll have more tasks to do, but it's closer to embracing adulthood: "Living in an apartment outside of campus also allows you to find your true identity apart from the college. You will be able to discover which things you like and dislike and shape a lifestyle out of them" (*5 perks of living in an apartment*, 2018).

How to Rent Your First Apartment

The renting process for apartments is way more complicated than for dorms. It's really an adulting task! Even my son Ethan, who is responsible and independent, couldn't rent his first apartment before his junior year despite his dad and I offering financial help. If you want to rent an apartment, the first thing to do is to estimate a realistic budget: There's no use in falling in love with a two-bedroom apartment with a terrace and indoor swimming pool if you won't be able to afford it later. If your budget is limited, you may want to consider getting a roommate to share the rent.

After finding an apartment that suits both your needs and your budget, you still have to follow a series of steps (Brown & Kho, 2023):

1. Complete a rental application. You'll provide your potential landlord with a series of documents and personal data, including your Social Security number for background checks, proof of ID, and income verification.

2. Pay the application fee. You'll need to pay between $30 and $50, and you won't get a refund if they deny your application for whatever reason.

3. Go through credit and background checks. The landlord

needs to make sure you are who you say you are and check your solvency, which, in simple words, means that you will be able to keep your word and pay the rent month after month. They will ask either for a solid credit score or for a cosigner—someone who signs the lease with you and accepts to take the responsibility if you fail to pay, it's a big responsibility that usually only very close family members are willing to take (Pirulis, 2019).

4. Provide references. They will ask you both for rental and personal references. You should let them know about your previous renting experiences, but if this is the first time you rent, give them contact numbers of people who can speak about your trustworthiness, such as your boss.

5. Pay your security deposit. You'll need to pay in advance an amount of money between one to three months of rent, which the landlord may keep if you trash the place.

6. Sign the lease and move into your new place!

Living With Others

Even if you live alone, you need to follow basic rules if you want to get along with your neighbors and avoid having problems with your landlord, such as respecting quiet hours (usually from 10 p.m. to 7 a.m. on weekdays, and up to 9 a.m. on weekends). This means no loud stereos, video games, TV, or parties. You also need to respect the time for hanging in the common areas, such as the patio or backyard, and the specific days and times for taking out the trash.

But when you live with a roommate, rules become even more important! Sharing your space with someone else is only possible if you both are comfortable. Otherwise, co-living will become a nightmare. And it doesn't matter if you move in with your best friend: Conflict will inevitably arise now and then. Some people decide to write them down and sign a roommate agreement, which, unlike a lease, isn't a legal obligation but can nonetheless get you both on the same page regarding your expectations.

What points should you include in your agreement? Here are some ideas:

• How to pay rent and expenses. Not only the price but also who's responsible for signing the check each month or how to split the bills (maybe your roommate does home office and can take a larger part of the Wi-Fi and electricity bills, for instance).

• How to handle the security deposit if the landlord retains part of it, or what's the requested notification if one of you wants to move before the end of the lease.

• If you are going to allow pets (of course, this also depends on the landlord accepting them).

• Agreeing on schedules and quiet hours. Perhaps one of you is a night owl who prefers to study up to 5 a.m. That's okay as long as the other one can sleep!

• Scheduling cleaning and other chores. Mention rules about food sharing and grocery shopping.

• Whether to accept visitors and sleepovers and for how long. You don't want your roommate's buddy to be a freeloader for a whole week!

• How to manage conflict in case one of you breaks the agreement in the future.

The best way to prevent arguments and discussions is to establish clear rules before moving in. If you find it too hard to agree on certain points or to negotiate, maybe you should evaluate if that person is the right roommate for you after all.

Table for One

If you are living in a dorm, there's a limit to how much cooking you can do. Anyhow, you probably signed up for a meal plan already. However, when living in an apartment, you must learn how to balance your grocery budget, the time you spend in the kitchen, and keeping a balanced diet. My son Ethan ate ramen for weeks when he first moved out, and he was desperately craving some good old homemade food!

Here are some tips to get you started on planning and preparing your meals. By the way, even a young teen who still lives with their family can make a huge contribution when implementing them.

Why Cook?

With so many fast food choices available just by touching your phone screen, why bother? Let me tell you, there are countless reasons why learning how to cook is a skill you shouldn't overlook!

- **It's better for your health:** When you cook, you control the ingredients that go into your food. Sure, you may add sugar, salt, or oil, but in limited amounts. The typical take-out food is full of unhealthy ingredients.
- **It's cheaper:** Preparing your food is way more economical than dining out, and still beats delivery when it comes to pricing. When living on a budget, cooking will help you stick to it while still eating delicious food.
- **It saves you time:** You may believe I'm wrong on this one, especially if you consider washing the dishes after every meal! But it happens that delivery is also time-consuming. If you plan and batch cook, you can stock your freezer with servings and have several meals ready for when you are busy studying for your midterms.
- **It allows you to try new stuff:** Take-out and delivery means you always eat the same dishes and the same ingredients. When it's you who cooks, you are more open to trying new flavors, and keeping a varied diet becomes easier.
- **It's empowering:** While at first, you may feel useless when your scrambled eggs get burned for the third time in a row, after a while, you'll feel you are mastering the art of cooking, and it will give you so much control over your life!
- **It's a great way of connecting with others:** Cooking allows you to bond with your loved ones. "Invite your friends and family over and stock the pantry with their favorite ingredients. You can cook multiple dishes from various different cuisines and have a true culinary adventure at home!" (Llobe, 2021).

Shopping and Storing

So, where to start? Begin by considering your personal preferences when it comes to meals. If you always drink coffee for breakfast, there's no point in investing in a box of fancy tea! Some basic supplies your pantry should always have are oil, salt and pepper, flour, eggs, sugar or other sweeteners, brown rice, oats, dried beans, nuts, assorted herbs, low-sodium broth, dry pasta, tortillas or taco shells, and some canned goods such as tuna or tomato sauce that can help you in an emergency.

Planning a weekly menu is the best way to save time, money, and mental energy. You'll notice that several meals take similar ingredients, and therefore, you can prepare them together! For example, if you want to grill vegetables on Monday and enjoy a casserole on Thursday, you can chop onions, carrots, and bell peppers in advance, and freeze half of them to have them ready for your second recipe.

Based on your menu, you'll come up with a shopping list. Before going to the supermarket and surrendering to your wildest impulses, make sure you eat something first (never go there hungry!) and stick to that list. Consider the basic nutritional groups we've seen before: Eating pasta is okay, but if you only feed yourself noodles and spaghetti, that's an excess of carbs and low in protein and fiber. Make sure you include plenty of fruits and vegetables—if possible, buy them fresh according to the in-season produce, if not, opt for frozen ones—meat, and dairy. And don't forget to always check the expiration dates.

When shopping, try to stay away from packaged foods as much as possible. They include lots of artificial ingredients and aren't the healthiest choices. Instead, buy *real* food: The chicken that a butcher cuts for you to grill is always better than those cheese-flavored nuggets.

You can find fresh fruits and veggies in a local farmer's market. Invite your friends to join you, so you can make a big purchase and save money! Most fruits and vegetables last for several days, but even the ones that don't can be frozen and saved for later.

Some meals are perfect for batch cooking! Casseroles, soups, pies, fillings you can use in many recipes, homemade sauce, even cookies... all of them can be stored for months and will taste just as good as when you first prepared them! However, this means having your freezer properly organized. Label your Tupperware to remember when each food was prepared, and always keep in the front whatever you need to eat first. Proteins go at the back, and fresh greens and produce go in the front. And defrost your freezer whenever you start noticing the ice layer getting thick, as this makes the freezer less effective.

By the way, not everything you buy should go into the fridge. Some fruits and vegetables are better out, such as tomatoes, bananas, mangos, and avocados, before they are ripe. Onions and potatoes should go somewhere dark and dry (a lower kitchen cabinet, for instance). It's important to do so, especially with potatoes, since exposure to light causes the buildup of the toxin solanine, which can cause vomiting and diarrhea if you eat them. Even if kept in the dark, rotten potatoes that have started to grow eyes release solanine gas, which can render a person unconscious when inhaled, or even kill if inhaled enough in a confined space (Jarvie, 2016).

You should always place dairy products such as milk, cheese, cream, butter, or yogurt; some fruits and vegetables such as apples, oranges, lemons, or salad greens; leftovers (for no more than one or two days!) and any container already opened in the fridge. This is because the fridge prevents bacteria from multiplying and getting you sick. For that same reason, meat, fish, or poultry go in the freezer unless you are planning to cook and eat them right away.

Whenever you are in doubt about a certain food that you forgot about, don't eat it! It's always better to be safe than sorry. Sure, throwing away food is a waste of time and money, but may it be a lesson to help you plan better for next time.

Keeping Your Place (Acceptably) Clean

Sure, if you are a student, there's a limited time you can dedicate to household chores. Guess what? The same happens to every single adult! We all have other duties, whether we are working full-time, taking care of our children, or organizing doctor appointments for other members of the family. Maintaining a house is never easy since it's an endless job!

However, you can learn how to organize yourself by prioritizing specific tasks and preventing a collapse. For instance, get used to putting everything in its place. When you come home from class, put your keys in their right spot, wipe or take off your shoes, hang your coat in the closet, put away your bag, and wash your hands. Keep clutter to a minimum!

Some cleaning tasks you'll need to do every day as part of your routine, such as making the beds, washing the dishes, wiping up spills, cleaning and disinfecting kitchen tops before and after preparing meals, or taking out the trash. Some other tasks should be done every other day, such as cleaning and disinfecting the bathroom "sink areas, toilet bowls, tubs, and showers to kill germs as well as mold and mildew that can trigger asthma attacks" (*Cleaning basics*, n.d.).

Some other cleaning tasks can be done once a week: Dusting shelves, vacuuming and mopping floors, or changing sheets and towels. Fun fact: 68 to 88 percent of dust in our homes are made up of our dead skin cells, as humans shed about 1.5 pounds of them per year (Smith, 2016). We are therefore literally cleaning up after ourselves! If you keep dirty clothes in a dry hamper, you can also organize a weekly laundry day—make sure to divide your clothes into whites and colors. There are even some tasks you can do monthly, such as cleaning windows, clearing your fridge, dusting the lightbulbs, washing the curtains, or wiping down walls.

Domestic Troubleshooting

To prevent costly repairs and serious trouble, this is what you should know before moving into a new place:

- Locate the fuse box, and learn how to cut the power.
- Find the inside stop valve to cut the flow of water in case there's a leak.

• Test and replace batteries in smoke and carbon monoxide detectors monthly.

• Learn how to use the fire extinguisher and check its expiration date monthly. Use a simple acronym **PASS** to remember how to operate most fire extinguishers. **Pull** to release the pin of the cylinder, **Aim** the nozzle at the base of the fire, **Squeeze** or press the handle, and **Sweep** side to side at the base of the fire until it goes out.

• As soon as a drain starts running slowly, unclog it with a mixture of vinegar and baking soda. Regularly running the hot water and with some detergent also helps clear the pipes.

Solving little domestic problems at home is part of adulting. While at first, you may run to call the janitor or the landlord for assistance at the slightest mishap, eventually, you'll learn to manage little emergencies by yourself, such as changing a lightbulb, fixing a running toilet, or unclogging a drain.

My children learned a few basic tricks for house maintenance by following their dad and me around as we worked things out. There's no better time to prepare yourself as an adolescent than while you still live with your parents. Ask them questions and seize every opportunity to learn! This may help you soon when it's your place that needs some fixing!

Chapter 3

Car Maintenance—And Other Ways to Travel

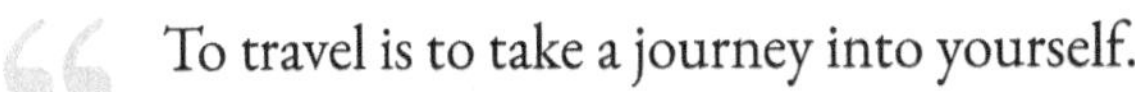 To travel is to take a journey into yourself.

— Danny Kaye, American actor, comedian, and humanitarian.

IT WASN'T until my son Lucas got his driver's license, the day after turning 16, when he told us about how he had been secretly saving money to buy his first car. Of course, pocket money and allowances wouldn't pay for a fancy Porsche or Mercedes, but still, he was so determined to get the four wheels that he wanted he was willing to get whatever he could afford! Luckily, we talked him out of accepting "a great deal" from a suspicious car dealer, and in the end, he didn't waste his hardly saved money on what looked like a piece of junk. He was mad at first but ended up thanking us later when he finally bought a secondhand, yet good, affordable Honda Civic that he still drives today.

Some teenagers aren't as lucky, and the urge to drive and own their first car leads them to impulsive purchases they later regret. In this chapter, we'll see what you need to know to become a conscious driver and car owner.

Getting Your Driver's License

Getting a learner's permit or driver's license is an important step in the life of every U.S. teen. Even if you can't afford a car yet, a driver's license is somehow a ticket into adulting, since it's also an ID document used for many other purposes. So, my first tip of the chapter is to get your driver's license as soon as you can. What does that mean? The requirements for the legal minimum age vary from state to state: While in Iowa, South Dakota, or Arkansas, the minimum entry age for the learner stage is 14, most states request the driver to be 16 years old for driving without supervision (*Driving age by state*, 2023).

Either by taking a driving course or by having a parent or an older sibling teach you, by all means, learn how to drive. My daughter Sophia is 15, and she's been driving ever since she turned 13, always supervised and in open spaces, but when the time comes, she'll be fully ready to get her license.

So, how do you get your driver's license? You should check the specific requirements and guidelines of your home state on the website of the local Department of Motor Vehicles (DMV). Generally

1. You take a vision test. Your license will state if you need to wear glasses or contacts when driving.

2. You provide proof of age and legal residency in the US.

3. You take a multiple-choice test. Read the driver's handbook and make sure you understand all the different rules and regulations.

4. You also need to prove that you know American road signs.

5. And finally, you take a practical driving test.

Most teens can obtain a learner's permit, which allows them to take courses and drive supervised before obtaining a full license. Again, the legal requirements vary according to the state of residence. And a final note regarding your license: Just remember that having a learner's permit is by no means an excuse for not respecting guidelines and traffic regulations everywhere—always drive safely.

Before You Buy Your First Car

Getting your first car is surely thrilling! But it's also a big investment and a huge responsibility. While at first, you may feel like giving in to impulse and buying that used convertible with a great stereo, you must consider some essentials before the purchase. If possible, don't make the decision alone: Ask an experienced friend or one of your parents to help you make up your mind. They may notice stuff you overlook because of the excitement of finally getting behind the wheel.

Decide on Your Budget

Before checking out cool models on car websites, you need to know what kind of car you can afford. As it happens in looking for an apartment to rent, it's no good falling in love with something out of reach! So, how do you set your budget? You have many options. My son Lucas first wanted to pay in cash with all of his savings. However, you can also take out a loan—which will give you more freedom of choice! Just make sure the car payments aren't above 10% of your monthly income (Axelton, 2020).

Paying for a car is one thing, affording a car is another! Buying a car is not like getting a video game console or a bicycle, you need to understand the lifetime cost of owning a vehicle. Consider that, besides gas, you'll also need to pay for regular maintenance, parking, and possible repairs. Other expenses are vehicle registration and car insurance, which we'll talk more about later on, but it's also mandatory in almost every U.S. state.

New or Second-Hand?

Used cars are traditionally cheaper than new models. However, they may not be worth it if you end up spending all that money on the mechanic! Besides, after the pandemic, the price proportion changed drastically: "If a used car is only \$1,000 less than the new model, it may be worth spending a bit extra for the newest features" (USAA, 2023). Also, consider that new cars come with a warranty and get better insurance policies.

If you still opt for a used car, purchasing it from a private seller is a big risk. If possible, get it from an acquaintance or someone with solid references—my son ended up getting my uncle's old car as he was certain of the vehicle's conditions—get the vehicle history report, and have it inspected by a mechanic (someone recommended by your family and friends of course, not by the potential seller) before you buy it. The mechanic may point at repairs that need to be done and those already made, traits of that specific car brand and model, small things that need immediate fixing, or possible future problems that may arise.

Know Your Future Car

Once you have set your eyes and your heart on a specific model, learn as much as possible about it. Research websites and read about the pros and cons of that specific make and model: "Whether it's a new or used model, investigate how well it's been performing and read any third-party reviews. It's also good to consider the vehicle's safety performance" (USAA, 2023).

You'll most likely find stuff that you don't like, but this doesn't mean you're not going to buy this car! Just make sure it fits into your needs and your lifestyle. For example, if a car tends to break easily when speeding but you're mainly going to drive near the college campus, then that's not a huge concern. At the same time, if a car is perfect for urban drivers but you need to go across the country because of your job, then you'd better keep looking for another model.

The test drive is also important for deciding, as it will allow you to see for yourself how the car feels and how it responds on the road. Taking a car for a spin before you buy it may help you decide whether it's the perfect car for you or not, even if it looks totally cool.

In the end, if you are still uncertain about investing all of that money in a car, you may consider leasing one. However, leasing is basically renting it: In the end, you'll have paid a monthly fee, but you won't own it.

Basic Car Maintenance

Once you become the proud owner of your first vehicle, you'll need to take care of it. Not only for saving money on potentially huge repairs but also for making sure you are not putting yourself and others at risk when taking your car on the road. Finding a mechanic you trust is essential, but you should also familiarize yourself with simple maintenance techniques and be alert for certain signs that something may be wrong.

• **Read the owner's manual.** Make sure you understand your vehicle's information system. It will also tell you how often the car should be checked and recommended services should be performed. Before driving your car, learn what the warning lights mean, as they may indicate anything from a mild problem you can check later to something serious that would need you to stop driving immediately.

• **Don't skip oil changes.** Traditionally, oil and filter changes happened every three months or 3,000 miles. But if you purchase a new car that uses synthetic oil, you may not need them as often: Once every 6–12 months or 5,000–10,000 miles may be enough (*Basic car maintenance tips*, n.d.)

• **Check the fluids.** Oil, radiation coolant, transmission fluid, brake fluid… Even if you regularly take the car to the mechanic for a fluid change, you should be able to check their levels and refill the fluids, if necessary, before your next checkup.

• **Check your tires.** Even brand-new tires lose air pressure with use, so you should learn how to check them periodically. "Always use the same tire pressure gauge and check the air pressure first thing in the morning, not after you've driven on them or they've been sitting in the hot sun" (*Car maintenance basics*, 2023). While we are at it, also measure the tire tread depth with an appropriate gauge. If you notice they are uneven, it's time to have the tires rotated and the car aligned. Another useful skill to practice is how to change a tire in case of an emergency.

• **Keep an eye on your battery.** While you are checking your car's fluids, take a look at the battery and look for signs of corrosion or buildup on its contacts, and if you notice any, use a cleaning brush. Car battery terminals that look corroded can also be easily fixed with a mixture of water and baking soda, and most car owners also learn how to jump-start a dead battery. The battery is an electric part of your vehicle, and you should know how to clamp the cables without getting any sparks. When in doubt, it's better to ask the pros.

Other useful skills include replacing wiper blades and headlights, checking the air filters, refilling the windshield washer fluid, and cleaning your car. But there's also a lot you can do to prevent problems with your car in the first place: Drive carefully, cover the car at night, and always the basic automotive tools—wrench set, jack, pliers, jumper cables, fluids, and electrical tape—with you when you drive.

Do I Really Need a Car?

While my two boys love their cars and consider them a major advantage of adulting, my daughter Sophia isn't as excited. Despite that she can already drive and she's willing to get her license as soon as she's old enough, she wonders whether buying a car and taking on so much trouble is actually worth it. I think this is due to her environmental concerns: She's one of those teens who worries about her carbon footprint and sustainability. I believe her worries are valid, and I'm pretty sure others share them as well.

Driving a car is a basic part of the American lifestyle for most U.S. teens, but depending on where you live, you may do well without one. For example, if you live in a city like New York or Boston, you may find that a car isn't the most convenient feature for moving around. In other countries of the world, fewer people are drivers, not necessarily because they can't afford cars, but because they don't need them as they are used to other means of transportation.

So, if you are anything like my daughter and you're wondering whether it's possible to be an adult and not own a car, the answer is *yes*. In the times of delivery and telecommuting, you may find that it suits your lifestyle better! Think about setting aside some of that money you are not spending on car loans, insurance, mechanics, or gas, and have a rainy day savings account.

And when you have to move around, here are your best alternatives to driving:

• **Public transport.** In other parts of the world, people who can afford a car still choose public transportation because they find it more convenient. And, although it may take a while for you to get used to your exact route and know how long it will take you, most U.S. cities offer buses with repetitive schedules.

• **Biking.** A bicycle is a great alternative for traveling short distances, although sometimes the weather makes it inconvenient. Besides saving lots of money and protecting the environment, regularly riding your bicycle to places is a great way to add plenty of aerobic exercise to your routine without having to schedule it!

• **Walking.** If you live in a big city such as New York, San Francisco, or Boston, you'll find most places are within walking distance: "You could expect to pay about $541 a month to park in Manhattan. If you can get yourself around town easily without a car, you can save some cash while adding to your daily step count" (*Could you live without a car*, 2018).

• **Carpooling.** It may be a great option for going to work or class every day. Find a colleague or a classmate who lives nearby and share with them the costs of gas, parking, and tolls. It's a win-win situation for both!

• **Car rental.** This is a great choice if you only need to drive occasionally (for example, when visiting your family on spring break). It's yet another reason to have your driver's license even if you don't plan to ever own a car.

• **Ridesharing.** Way safer than hitchhiking and more affordable than traditional taxis, apps like Uber or Lyft became game-changers for nondrivers. You should always consider them when you go to parties, and there's a chance you may drink: Remember to never drive under the influence, not only because you risk getting a ticket or your license taken away, but mostly because you could end up injuring yourself or others.

As we've seen, having a car is a major decision when it comes to embracing adulthood. And one choice that you shouldn't take lightly is how you're going to afford and maintain it. Our next chapter will be all about money, by the way!

Chapter 4

Money Skills—'Cause We Are Living in a Material World

> It's not about how much money you make, but how much money you keep and how hard it works for you.
>
> — Robert Kiyosaki, personal finance expert and author of *Rich Dad Poor Dad.*

IF YOU ARE like most teens, you probably consider learning about money one of the most important adulting skills to master. Whether you grew up in a comfortable home, with parents who could fulfill all of your material desires, or if your family struggled to make ends meet, you may know by now that being independent means also knowing how to get money, save money, and spend it wisely.

In this chapter, we'll have a closer look at ways you can save even before getting a full-time job, some words and concepts you must know before diving into adulthood, and tips for creating a balanced budget, among other things.

Financial Jargon for Newbies

Does it ever happen to you that when you hear your parents or other adults talking about money, it stresses you out because there are so many terms you don't understand? What seemed uninteresting when you were in your early teens becomes a concern as you start to realize it *will* have to do with you and your life—or it already does!—and it *is* likely to affect you whether you care about it or not. After all, if you don't understand how to use money, you may end up making poor decisions.

I asked my children and some of their classmates what are some of the most difficult words or concepts they wish their teachers would teach them at school; here are the ones related to finances. I hope it helps!

Account

Think about it as the "place" in a financial institution—a bank or a credit union—where you "put" your money to be safe. While a **checking account** gives you quick access to your funds and, therefore, allows you to pay your bills or buy stuff, a **savings account** is meant for, that's right, saving. This means you need to keep your money there for a specific time frame, and depending on the bank, you can't withdraw it all at once. The good thing about a savings account is that the bank pays you monthly **interest** (an extra amount that makes your savings grow) as compensation for lending them your money.

Compound Interest

If simple interest is that extra amount you receive or pay for the money you either lend or borrow, compound interest is "interest on interest" that accumulates (Landry, 2018). This is what makes certain **investments** so attractive, but at the same time, makes debt such a huge financial risk.

Credit Card

It is basically a **loan** that a financial institution offers to customers who qualify for it. What they look for is someone likely to pay off their debts, in other words, someone with a solid **credit score**. Therefore, when you use your plastic to pay for goods and services or to take a cash advance, you are committing yourself to paying the financial institution that issued the credit card later.

The longer you take to complete your payments, the more you pay in interest, that's why you should attempt to pay your whole balance every month. When credit cardholders are unable to pay off their debt, interest accumulates, making this debt higher as months go by. Many people in the US deal with this problem (Haagensen, 2023).

Credit Score

It's a number banks and credit companies use to see if you qualify for a loan, and for which amount. In the US, most people and institutions use the FICO Score, although there are other credit bureaus as alternatives.

A credit score usually falls in the range of 300–850, and the higher your score, the better the chances of obtaining a loan and paying less interest. They get this number by looking at your credit report, which evaluates your history of paying bills on time, if you ever asked for loans before, how long it took for you to pay them, whether you have an existing debt already, if you have already applied to credit elsewhere, and similar stuff.

Debit Card

Like credit cards, it's a little plastic rectangle with numbers and your name on it. But this time, it only gives you access to money in your account. Debit cards are a convenient way to avoid carrying cash: Most stores accept them as a payment method, and you can also use them at the automated teller machine (**ATM**) to get cash. Debit cards are convenient and have largely replaced checks as they are easier to use.

Inflation

This word defines an overall increase in the price of goods and services that happens over time. Sometimes, it can occur because of a sudden shock to the economic system, for example, during the

COVID-19 pandemic: "If things cost more but your income doesn't increase to match the rise in prices, then your money is worth less than it was before because it can't purchase as much as it used to be able to buy" (Haagensen, 2023).

Investment

Imagine you keep your money in a piggy bank. Next time you check, no matter how long it takes, there will be the exact same amount of money you placed there. On the contrary, making an investment is putting your money somewhere that is likely to produce *more* money in the future. For example, if you invest in website domain names that later you sell for a higher price, a collectible that appreciates some years later, or the stock market.

However, investments don't guarantee you'll make more money, and you may end up losing some instead. For example, that Superman collectible you thought was going to be a hit on eBay doesn't get any offers after the movie bombs. In general, the higher the risk, the higher the profit you get if the investment succeeds. When investing, the more informed you are of the possible risks and motifs while it may succeed, the better. People make a career out of investing smartly!

Return on Investment (ROI)

It is a calculation used to determine how likely an investment, such as a good, a project, or an activity, is to pay back what you invested in the first place. For example, if you buy a bicycle to ride to class and work, you can estimate the ROI by calculating how much you are saving yourself on public transport and how long it will take this saving to match the price you paid for such a bike.

Taxes

It is the money that the government collects and uses to pay for the collective good, "such as building and maintaining infrastructure (e.g., roads, bridges, subway systems), running schools, fielding a military, and providing social programs" (Haagensen, 2023). It is mandatory to pay taxes to federal, state, and local governments. We'll see more about this coming on.

Where Your Money Goes

Even when you were a little child and bought a candy bar at the store, you were paying taxes without knowing. And the older you get, the more financial obligations you have. As soon as you start earning your own money, you need to attend to it! So, let's see where your money ends up besides getting cool stuff or paying for concert tickets.

Types of Taxes and How and When to Pay Them

We've already given the basic definition of taxes. You should also know that there are different types of taxes that you may need to pay. Being a teen or a young adult, you should care about the following three at the moment:

• **Income tax:** It's money that gets deducted from your paycheck. You pay it automatically every month or whenever you get paid by your employer. The more you earn, the higher taxes you pay proportionally. But other factors affect your taxes as well, for example, whether you're single or married.

• **Sales tax:** It's money that gets paid every time someone buys certain goods or services. You pay them at the point of sale—for instance, the cash register at the supermarket. In the US, each state establishes its own sales tax, which partially explains why stuff can be more expensive in certain places than in others.

• **Property tax:** It's money you pay for having properties, such as an apartment. Not only do you pay taxes when you first purchase them, but you keep paying them annually, usually in April. Some states also tax personal property, such as cars.

In the US, the institution responsible for collecting federal income taxes is the Internal Revenue Service (IRS). Failing to pay your taxes results in different penalties. However, most young adults aren't concerned about this type of tax (yet): "Federal income tax legislation usually only pertains to people who have earned a certain amount of income or adjusted gross income" (Gorton, 2023).

College Expenses

College isn't cheap! The average cost for attending a public institution and living on campus for four years is $26,027 per year or $104,108 over four years, and even more if you are attending a school out of state. Private institutions cost twice as much. Not to mention that only two out of five students graduate in that time frame! This cost has doubled in the past few decades (Hanson, 2023). And if that isn't enough, you must include supplies (such as books and technology), transportation, meal plans, and other things. It's a whole lot of money, especially considering that students are unable to get full-time jobs while attending their courses.

While some families can help with college funds they've been saving ever since the child was born, maybe this isn't the case. And you are not alone. Each year, 34% of U.S. students borrow money to pay for college expenses. Of course, as with any other loan, this money has to be paid back, something usually done by the time you graduate. As with any other loan, interest accumulates, which means the more you borrow and the longer you take to pay it back, the more you'll owe.

You can opt for two types of student loans: federal or private. Federal student loans are more affordable than private ones. You apply for them through the Free Application for Federal Student Aid (FAFSA), which requires no credit score and offers some benefits for the future. Only if you're not eligible should you consider a more expensive private loan. It's advisable that you accept the minimum you need for college and not as much as you can get. "One rule of thumb is to borrow the amount that will keep your student loan payments around 10% of your projected after-tax monthly income" (Helhoski, 2021). Also, consider that a student's loan is not cash on hand: You can only use it to pay it for certain college expenses—no, that doesn't include spring break in Florida! —and most times, the loan is directly paid to your school.

Student loans mean that you'll be paying for college for many years, even after graduating. Private loans usually request earlier payments, while federal loans offer you more flexibility. In any case, failing to pay your student loan comes with dreadful consequences for your financial future.

A way to avoid ending up full of debt is by getting a scholarship. Unlike a student loan, the money you get from a scholarship doesn't have to be paid back, which is a huge relief both to you and your family! Different institutions offer scholarships both to prospective and previously enrolled students. Some of these scholarships consist of a one-time payment, while others are renewable, which means students get paid annually or per semester. Besides paying for college expenses such as tuition and room and board, you can use the money to buy books and other fees.

So, how can you get a scholarship? Most times, they depend on academic merit, which means you have to obtain excellent grades and maintain them to benefit from them. Your grades and your general behavior should remain spotless if you want to keep your scholarship. Scholarships may also mean future work and academic opportunities.

From all points of view, scholarships provide a great opportunity for all students, but particularly for those that come from less privileged backgrounds, as they can make a difference in their lives: "Most families might not be able to send their children to higher institutions but a scholarship can make higher education possible for anyone who meets the specific eligibility criteria" (Scholarships, n.d.).

Insurances

Insurance is a service provided by financial institutions where you pay a regular amount of money (a premium) to cover unexpected expenses, such as health problems, car or property damage, or legal problems. You pay some money ahead of time to save yourself from paying a huge amount of money if any unexpected event should happen in the future. This means it's kind of a seatbelt for your finances (Wei, 2022).

As a teen, you're likely to have your parents paying insurance for you—your health insurance policy, for instance. But as you become an adult, you'll need to make that decision on your own. You may need mandatory car insurance, or home or rental insurance if you rent your first apartment.

Also, even when you are young, you may be eligible for life insurance, which means that in the event of your death, your loved ones receive some money to protect them from financial collapse. Some people decide to take this kind of policy after starting a family. Note that the amount you pay varies depending on your health condition, so a young adult who doesn't drink and smoke, who exercises, and who has a good medical history is not likely to pay much.

How to Save Money Way Before Turning 18

Just like you should learn basic household skills before moving on your own, you should also have some savings set aside for all those big expenses coming ahead as you grow up. Whether for a car initial payment, for the deposit of your first rented apartment, or for traveling abroad, you should do your best to save as much money as possible before turning 18.

Of course, because you're just a teen, this means your sources of income are limited. That's why it's more important than ever to avoid throwing your money away on impulsive purchases and consider it as an investment for your future. Does being responsible sound boring? It doesn't need to be, as long as you keep a big goal ahead: To be a successful, thriving young adult who can fulfill their life goals!

When and How Much to Save

It's never too early to start saving some money. Even from elementary school or middle school, you should set aside most of what you receive from presents, pocket money, allowances, etc. The rule of thumb should be to save whatever extra money you have unless you have a specific purchase already in mind. For example, if you were looking forward to buying new headphones and you count on your birthday approaching instead of asking your parents, it's okay to spend that paycheck from your aunt. However, if you happen to receive a present and you are not sure what to buy with that money, then by all means, save it!

Another useful method, especially once you have a steady income, is the 50/20/30 split recommended by the website *Money Under 30* (Weliver, 2023): 50% of your income goes to paying fixed expenses (guitar lessons, your gym membership, or a contribution at home if your parents are struggling), 30% is for you to enjoy as you wish, and the remaining 20% goes to savings. Later on in this chapter, we'll discuss how opening more than one account can help you reach this goal.

But what if money seems to slip right out of your hands? What if you never manage to set aside some savings because you are using your paycheck to pay back to your friends or your parents from the last time you borrowed some cash? Then, it's time to evaluate your current expenses and make some cuts. For example

• If your friends always hang out at the food court after school, you can eat food you've packed at home and only buy a soda. You'll save money while you still get to spend time with your friends.

• If most of your paycheck goes to taking an Uber, maybe you can switch to riding your bike to nearby places.

• Hide your credit and debit card and use only cash. You'll find you don't spend as much when you see the money going bye-bye!

• If you are tempted to buy that cool t-shirt because you saw it's on sale, ask yourself whether you'd still be buying it if it was full price. Chances are it's an impulsive purchase, and you don't really need it!

• Buy secondhand. You can find all kinds of products—from clothes to tech, from board games to books—at a much more affordable price. Plus, it's better for the environment!

Money Sources

Once you manage to get your first part-time job, you need to understand your income, because what you get paid and the money you actually get are two different things: "When you get a paycheck, you need to know how much money you'll get both before and after taxes—also known as separating gross income from net income" (Weliver, 2023). The same applies to hidden expenses such as tips, bonuses, and discounts. When my son Lucas found his first job at a fast food place, he was thrilled to find out it also included a cool discount—that was until more than half of his paycheck was spent paying for those "free" burgers he gave to some of his friends!

Maybe you're still too young to find a job in retail or serving fries and burgers, but I bet there are still plenty of things you can do to get some cash. My son Ethan used to tutor younger students. My daughter Sophia sells pictures of food and other objects on image databases online. As for Lucas, my young entrepreneur, he has taken all kinds of part-time jobs. Besides the burger place, he also tried lawn mowing, walking the neighbors' dogs, delivering pizzas, and babysitting (yes, a boy babysitter *is* possible). Lucas has a motto regarding money: *If something takes a little bit of effort, someone will always be willing to pay someone else for doing it.* So far, he's the only one of my children who has managed to save enough to start a small business, which he's planning to do as soon as he graduates from high school, so he may have a point!

Why and How to Save?

Do you remember when you were little, and the Tooth Fairy visited you? Whenever you found a dollar under your pillow, you used to stash it in a can or a piggy bank. If you've read this far, you know that they aren't the best choices: Saving cash or checks won't give you any interest, your money may lose some of its value because of inflation, and what's even more important, having the money at an arm's distance is almost a guarantee you'll end up spending it on impulsive purchases.

That's why the first thing you need to save is a savings account —remember that, unlike a checking account, it requires you to leave your money for a specific period, but in exchange, it pays you back monthly interest that adds to the total amount you manage to save.

Opening a Savings Account

When you are a teen living with your parents, you probably won't have a bank of your own. Still, your folks could help you out since most financial institutions offer students' and teens' savings accounts, which are great ways to get you started (Oh, 2022). Ask Mom or Dad to assist you in making your first deposit whenever you receive money as a birthday gift.

Once you find your first job, some employers offer direct deposit, which means your salary goes straight to a bank account instead of being paid in cash. However, a checking account is not the best way to save. You should split your money and set up an automatic deposit into a savings account. This means that whenever you get paid, a fraction of your money goes straight into savings without you having to put it away. This is a great practice not just for teens, but for anyone willing to be consistent when saving for a future financial goal.

How Many Accounts Do You Need?

While splitting your money into a checking account and a savings account is the basic thing to do, some experts suggest it's even better to have five, or at least three different accounts (Browning, 2021). In this way, you can establish the 50/30/20 rule we mentioned earlier:

• Open one checking account for bills (50% of your income goes to this checking account for needs and fixed expenses). For example, paying your bills, paying your French tutor, gas or bus rides, groceries, and similar expenses.

• Open another checking account for your lifestyle (30% of your income goes to this second checking account for wants and short-term saving goals). For example, going to the cinema, buying concert tickets, or getting a new iPhone. You should aim to increase the monthly ledger balance for this account to nurture good spending habits and not spend everything.

• Finally, open a savings account for emergency funds (20% of your income goes for emergency funds and, after that, for long-term savings goals). For example, saving for the initial car payment, fixing a leaking pipe, or having knee surgery—hopefully, you won't need any, but if it happens, it could have dreadful financial consequences.

While you are at it, try not to keep all three accounts in the same bank: "In case technology fails at one institution, for example, you have accounts at other banks to fall back on" (Browning, 2021). And remember to keep track of your savings and expenses using any of the free budgeting apps available.

Do I Need an Emergency Fund?

When living with your parents, you may not feel the direct impact of unexpected financial emergencies as they are always there to help you out. But being an adult means facing the consequences of sudden, unplanned expenses that often hit us at the worst possible times: Your dog destroyed the carpet in your apartment, your phone broke, or your car's brakes need to be replaced.

Think about it: What would you do if a sudden expense came up? You may need to borrow money from your parents, but what if they can't lend it to you? Paying with a credit card will cost you way more in the long term, the same as asking for a loan. Both of them could impact your credit score, which means you'll face the consequences for years to come.

The emergency fund comes as a way of rescuing you in these situations that otherwise cause you to fall into serious debt: "By putting money aside—even a small amount—for these unplanned expenses, you're able to recover quicker and get back on track toward reaching your larger savings goals" (*An essential guide*, n.d.). As we've seen, automatic recurring transfers into a savings account are the best way to commit yourself to saving. This is especially important if you lack a consistent monthly income.

So, let's imagine you did the right thing and you already have quite an amount saved. How long should you keep saving until you can, you know, *enjoy* your hard-earned money without thinking of ambulance bills and other disasters? For example, once you manage to put aside six months' income for your emergency fund, come up with a money goal and stick to it! Start saving for that trip to the Bahamas or for that cool motorbike.

Creating a Sustainable Budget

We've discussed how to face unexpected expenses. Now let's talk about your regular ones. What's the best way to administrate your money to avoid spending more than you earn? You need to create a budget, which you can do one step at a time. While at first, it may sound restraining, a budget is not a restriction but a plan on how to spend your money: "When you learn how to make a budget—and do it every month—you're giving your money purpose. You're taking control. Goodbye, money anxiety. Hello, money goals" (*How to make a budget*, 2023).

Creating a Budget

The first thing to do is list your monthly income: How much do you get from your paycheck after taxes are deducted? Do you get any other income, maybe from small chores you do at home, or from mowing the neighbor's yard? Make sure you list them all. If your income is irregular, keep track of the money you've received in the past three or four months and calculate the average.

Secondly, list where your money goes: Include every expense you have, such as food, transportation, shelter, and utilities. As a young adult, you may list bills, insurance, rent, or student loans. Don't forget to add savings to the list!

Now, you subtract your expenses from your income. You have three options:

• **You have money left over.** This means you aren't spending or saving everything you earned. Be careful not to waste this remaining money on coffee, candy, or impulsive online purchases! Put this money to work: Make an investment, add it to your money goal, or consider giving some to charity.

• **You have a zero-based budget.** If there's only a little buffer in your bank account, this means you're doing things right! You're dividing your money into spending and saving, and you'll be able to reach your goals.

• **You have a negative number.** Okay, now it's time to cut expenses. Thanks to your list, you know exactly where your money goes. Think about cooking at home instead of eating out or buying second-hand clothes until you can afford those fancy brands.

What You Can Do With Tech

Many budgeting apps allow you to create and track your budget month after month. While you could always try to get a free app, consider that being free, it doesn't get updated with new features or catch up with OS compatibility updates. Plus, expense tracking becomes more useful the longer one uses it.

Thus, you need to find a good app with all the needed features, that is in for the long run, that you stick with and not switch out (which is hard to, anyway). Here are some of them:

• **Mint:** Although it's the most popular free app for budgeting, you should know that the company uses your information to show you ads and may track your data for other purposes. Or, as my son Lucas puts it, while you're technically not paying them, you're offering something more valuable in exchange for their app.

• **Simplifi by Quicken:** With an annual subscription of $48, it offers a simple, intuitive interface and a user-friendly design. You can sync your bank accounts and come up with a personalized spending plan.

• **You Need a Budget (YNAB):** More expensive and complex than Simplifi, it's a valuable tool for people who attempt a zero-based budget. It offers a steep learning curve, and it's a way to train your brain to spend less (Pinola & Tepper, 2023).

Throughout this chapter, we've seen a general overview of money matters that you need to consider as you enter adulthood, although it's never too soon to learn! My three children started their savings account by the time they were 14. Ethan managed to go to college with just an affordable loan, Lucas is saving for his startup, and Sophia hasn't decided on her money goal yet, but she's got used to saving every birthday check she gets from her grandparents—that unless she has the chance to go to a Taylor Swift concert nearby, of course!

The following chapter will be about managing another priceless resource that, more often than not, seems scarce. We're talking about time.

Chapter 5

Time Management—How to Make the Best of It

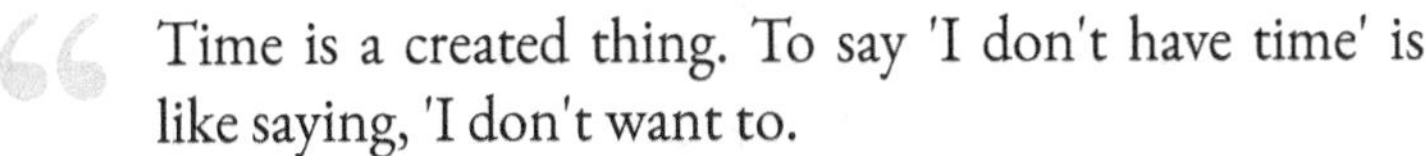

Time is a created thing. To say 'I don't have time' is like saying, 'I don't want to.

— Lao Tzu, ancient Chinese philosopher and author of the *Tao Te Ching*.

I REMEMBER when Ethan was in middle school. Although he was a great student, more often than not, I ended up apologizing on his behalf for missing a deadline (sometimes it was just an hour!). He seemed to be always running around doing his chores, riding his bike to hockey practice, or being late when he had to meet with his classmates. Luckily for him, his father and I were still in charge of scheduling his dentist appointments and driving him there; otherwise, he would still have his braces on now in his 20s.

It wasn't until he started high school that he understood the importance of time management. One of his professors refused to accept a late assignment in which he had worked hard, and he had to face the consequences: It was his first and last F on one of his report cards. From then onwards, he decided he needed a change.

If you, like Ethan and so many teenagers, feel like the day doesn't last long enough for everything you have to do, if hours and minutes seem to slip by without you being aware, you could use time management skills. In this chapter, we'll see why you should think of the 24 hours of your day as 24 opportunities and seize them the best you can.

The Importance of Organizational Skills

Some teens—as well as some adults—seem to never finish anything on time. Their "to-do" lists are always overloaded, and nothing they manage to complete is enough as new tasks keep piling up. If this happens to you, it may be because you simply are taking too much on your hands and you need to take a break, but most likely, it's because you have yet to develop some basic organizational skills.

Learning how to organize yourself is not only useful for handing in your school papers, but also for keeping your household chores done, being on time when you meet with your friends, doing great at any job, and basically, living a life with less stress and worries. Some people have a natural gift for organizing, but if this isn't your case (I can say it's not mine either!), don't worry: Anyone can acquire organizational skills with self-discipline and practice. As it happens with taking care of yourself, it's a matter of creating new habits.

Organizational skills are important because they help you structure and put in order your daily life: "They can help you work more efficiently and effectively and, as a result, increase your productivity and performance" (Birt, 2022). A lack of organization for a student usually means they get distracted easily, get poorer grades, and have more negative interactions with their teachers. On the other hand, people who display solid organizational skills manage to complete their tasks on time, set clear goals, and meet them consistently and effectively using their energy.

So, where can you start? Let's begin by learning about some organizational skills examples and how to implement them. However, don't feel overwhelmed! You won't improve everything at once. Try to focus on those skills you consider most important for your particular personality, the things you find more challenging. Even a small improvement in your organization is likely to produce amazing results.

Everything in Its Place

The first thing you can do to start developing new organizational habits is to organize your personal space. That's right: Clutter—both physical and virtual—interferes with thought, distracts you, and takes away precious time from your hands (think about how many minutes you waste looking for that old file you need to submit). Clear your laptop desk and create folders for each class or project. Label your files so you can access them later. As for your desk at home, make sure you remove all unnecessary items and put them away, or throw them in the trash if they belong there!

And while we are speaking about places, do you have a designated area to study or to work? Having a clear, organized space will help your brain work more effectively. If you don't have an area, choose one and make sure it's clean and organized. It may help you to add some furniture and a few decorations that you like, because the more motivated you feel to remain in such a space, the more you'll dedicate yourself to keeping it neat. Take a few minutes before each work or studying session to tidy up your workspace (Sippl, 2020).

Finally, space organization skills are also about your papers and assignments. Make sure you hand in or forward a paper only after properly formatting it, including titles and subtitles, a content page, and possibly a cover. When you attend a work meeting, your notes or presentations should be clear and logically organized to better communicate with your colleagues or your superiors.

Making Lists and Assigning Priorities

Get used to writing down everything that you need to do. This will help you visualize the priorities and remove them from your mental load. However, an endless to-do list won't help you complete the most important tasks on time unless you organize it. First, divide your list into tasks that you need to perform every day and those that you should do once a week, or maybe just once. You can use different fonts or colors for this.

Second, assign priorities to each item on your list. For example, changing the brake fluid on your car is more important than taking it to the car wash. You can also sort out the list based on deadlines and appointments, and leave for later those tasks that you can do at any time. You wouldn't skip an appointment with your dentist to do laundry, the same way you wouldn't be late for a job interview because it's been forever since you had your nails done.

What about larger projects that seem endless, such as preparing a presentation? Start by considering how long it may take you to reach the final deadline, then break the project up into smaller tasks, and that's what you'll write in your to-do list. "You might also assign due dates to your tasks to help you stay on track. This can help you complete larger projects without feeling overwhelmed" (Birt, 2022).

The OHIO Rule

Those small, specific tasks you sometimes leave for later because they seem unimportant may take an awful lot of time and energy as you postpone them and go back to them over and over again: "For years, process engineers and organization experts have touted the OHIO Rule or "Only Handle It Once" for specific tasks like email, paperwork, and homework" (Sippl, 2020).

Sending a brief confirmation email, washing the cup after you finish your coffee, or printing that report will take only a few minutes, and then you can forget all about it as it's already done.

Rewarding Yourself

Self-motivation is super important for building new habits. When it comes to your organizational skills, you can come up with a reward system to encourage consistency. For instance, every day that you manage to tackle all the items in your daily to-do list, treat yourself! It could be listening to some music, eating a piece of chocolate, or taking a long, relaxing shower: "When you acknowledge your achievements, even in small ways, it can help you build motivation to complete each project. This can build a productive work cycle for yourself and can encourage you to remain organized" (Birt, 2022).

Creating a Schedule

Time is limited, and sometimes, the busier you are, the less productive you feel. Don't you ever get that sensation you are trapped in a loop of endless tasks and interruptions, and you never get to do what's important? If you do, then you will benefit from scheduling. This is the task that allows you to effectively plan your activities and your goals in the time you have available.

Benefits of Scheduling

We can't buy time, and that's why it seems such a scarce resource more often than not. But when you learn how to schedule and plan your day, your week, your month, and your year, you get all of these advantages (*Effective scheduling*, n.d.):

• Get an understanding of what you can achieve with the time you have.

• Be realistic and avoid taking on more than you can handle.

• Save time for essential tasks.

• Consider "the unexpected" and add contingency time.

• Keep a steady rhythm of work or study to reach your goals.

• Keep a healthy work-life balance and have time for being with your loved ones, exercise, and do whatever you like.

Best Scheduling Tools

Creating a schedule doesn't have to be complicated. The first thing you have to do is choose the appropriate tool that works best for you. Some people prefer visuals, such as a big calendar with magnets they can hang on the wall. Others carry notebooks, journals, calendars, and other physical tools. Nowadays, most teens and young adults will probably prefer digital apps. Any of those tools will work just fine, and perhaps it may help you to use more than one. For example, you can use a calendar to schedule single-time tasks, and an app on your phone as a reminder of daily tasks.

Using a schedule maker offers many benefits, such as relieving your stress, enhancing your productivity, and learning to prioritize. Besides, most virtual scheduling tools are excellent for including others on the same schedule and making sure everyone involved is on board—for example, when booking a studying session, private tutoring, or a video call.

Here's a list of schedule makers you can start using. The best news is all of them are free!

• **Google Calendar** is a simple tool that takes up little space in your phone. You can schedule single-time or regular tasks, include virtual meeting links, and send invitations to other users so they can add the task to their own schedule.

• **ClickUp** is a productivity app many managers and students use to better organize themselves. It's easy to customize and offers different views of your daily schedule and workload.

• **Asana** is a tool for project management, as it allows you to break up projects into smaller tasks and assign them to the people in charge (great for teamwork!). Its timeline is a great feature for time management.

• **Canva** is a tool for those who like strong visual designs. You can customize schedule sheets with your personal preferences and then download them for printing. Another choice if you like pen and paper is Calendarpedia.

• **Evernote** is a useful app for those who prefer to keep their desk as paper-free as possible. Some of its features include scanning documents, searching, web clipping, and synchronizing notes and calendars. It has a free plan but also premium paid ones.

How to Create a Schedule Step-By-Step

Once you've explored some scheduling tools and you have decided on an option, how do you use it effectively? Try assigning a fixed day and time for scheduling: For example, you can plan your week every Sunday evening, or plan the day the night before. Here are some easy steps to follow:

1. Start by identifying your available time. The day has 24 hours, but you need to sleep, eat, and take care of yourself. *How* you distribute your availability is up to you: Perhaps you're a night owl, and you don't mind scheduling a task at 2 a.m. Decide how many hours you'll dedicate to your work, studies, and essential household chores.

2. Schedule the absolutely essential. That includes classes you are taking, your work time, or job interviews already confirmed that you can't easily reschedule.

3. Choose the best time for your high-priority tasks. Look at your to-do list and make room in your schedule for those activities you must complete and that you can't delegate. The best time for these are those parts of the day when you feel you're the most productive: "Some people are at their most energized and efficient in the morning, while others focus more effectively in the afternoon or evening" (*Effective scheduling*, n.d.).

4. Schedule time for the unexpected. This may sound counterintuitive. How can you schedule something that is not supposed to happen? What we mean is that you always need to schedule some extra time to deal with contingencies, knowing that, if you don't, emergencies will still happen, and you'll find yourself overwhelmed by them.

5. Schedule your personal goals. Whatever blank spaces you have left in your scheduling tool is discretionary time, which means those hours—or days, or maybe minutes!—you have to do whatever pleases you the most. Don't just leave them empty; otherwise, you'll risk wasting them on scrolling through your phone. Schedule whatever you need to reach personal goals: It may be writing on your blog, working out, talking to a friend, or batch-cooking for the rest of the week.

6. Schedule a "Thinking Time" each day. Set aside time for reflection and contemplation of important but not urgent aspects of your work and life. This can lead to increased clarity on goals and priorities, and more focused and innovative approaches to problem-solving. The more time you spend thinking, the less time you need to spend on doing, and the more intentional your life becomes.

If, by the time you reach the final step, you realize you have little to no time left, it may be time to analyze your activities and decide if all the tasks you included are indeed necessary. Maybe some can be delegated (for instance, you and your roommate take turns doing laundry), and maybe some should be skipped (perhaps you were too optimistic when you signed up for all of those optional classes).

It's the same as we learned about budgeting your money in Chapter 4, only with hours. You only have a limited amount of time: You need to decide how to make the best out of what you have.

"Getting Things Done"

Productivity consultant David Allen (2015) published a book called *Getting Things Done*, which became a bestseller and, later, a whole time management system millions of people worldwide have chosen to improve their productivity, both at work and with their personal goals.

Allen observed that our brains are more effective when processing information than when keeping it. Therefore, the GTD method relies on the principle of decluttering your mind from information, interests, pending tasks, issues, and projects. By recording them externally and sorting them into a list of actionable tasks, you can later focus on each item one by one.

These are the five essential steps the method proposes (Allen, 2015):

1. Capture: The first thing to do is collect everything that has caught your attention. What's on your mind right now? Do you need to call the plumber? Pay your car insurance? Change your career? Take a trip to Mexico? Or perhaps read the latest Stephen King novel? Write *everything* down! You can use pen and paper, although there are plenty of GTD tools available, such as Todoist or Notion.

2. Clarify: Once you have the list, decide on whether each item is actionable. If it's something that can be done in less than two minutes, do it (remember the OHIO rule!). If it's something that requires more than one step, then you'll consider it as a project.

Other stuff may be references or something you can put on hold for some time. This depends on your particular circumstances: A trip to Mexico can be either a distraction—if you are in the middle of your semester and should be working on your paper—or a project to fulfill—if you've been saving for that purpose and summer vacation is approaching.

3. Organize: Put everything in its right place. Sort your tasks, delegate whatever you can, file away reference materials, schedule dates in your calendar, and so on. Following the same example, choose a date for your trip, book airline tickets, read hotel reviews, and do whatever else you need to do.

4. Reflect: Take the habit of periodically looking over, updating, and revising your lists. You may find some of them are no longer necessary! Perhaps you read a poor review of a book, and now you no longer want to read it. By all means, move them to the trash can or erase them from your list.

5. Engage: Get to work on the next important task. The system will allow you to visualize what you should be doing at any specific time. Instead of telling yourself that you have to book the tickets, go to the airline website and *book* them.

GTD doesn't request a specific tool, application, or product to be implemented, as long as you respect its principles of clearing your mind and extracting every thought, task, or pending assignment onto something external. However, many followers of this methodology find online tools particularly useful. For example, the Notion GTD Template is a basic online tool you can use to start implementing this system. It allows you to create pages for the following:

• **Inbox:** For capturing all you are considering, from ideas you have for future projects, to pending household tasks and everything in between. "Anytime you have an idea—add it here. Then, once a week, review and process your inbox" (Davies, 2023).

• **Projects:** Here, you break up big goals into smaller steps (more on this later on).

• **Next actions:** Things that you have to get to work on, organized by priority. Alternatively, any small task that you listed in your inbox that needs less than two minutes should be completed right away.

• **Read/review:** Here, you list articles, books, and bibliographies, that either you must read to complete your project, or you'd like to read.

• **Someday/maybe:** This is for listing potential future projects that you can't deal with right away, but still would like to consider shortly.

Ever since Ethan embraced the GTD system through the Notion application on his mobile phone, he has successfully regained control over all his to-do tasks. In doing so, he discovered that he was gradually building a comprehensive database encompassing records of his social interactions, health symptoms, books he has read, items he has purchased, and even journaling! With every piece of data fastidiously organized within Notion, Ethan has gained a better grasp of his habits and preferences. He finds himself gaining deeper insights of who he is, enabling him to make significant strides in every facet of his life. He is more motivated now that he sees how each task aligns with a specific project, each project serves as a stepping stone towards either a short-term or long-term goal, and every goal contributes meaningfully to the overarching vision he holds for his life. There is now meaning and purpose in his daily tasks, as he would say to me.

Dreams, Goals, Plans, and Steps

What's your biggest dream?

You may find the question childish in a book about adulting, but the truth is that any person who has achieved something big has dreamed about it first. And giving up on their dreams is what makes some adults bitter, disappointed, and unmotivated with their lives. Being a teen or a young adult, I bet you have some big dreams, and accepting this is the only life you get, you'd better do something to make them come true! So, dream big. And then, do something about it.

How can we make our dreams come true when they seem impossible? It won't be easy, but you can achieve them if you turn a dream into a plan and put your energies into achieving every step of it toward a clear, effective, measurable goal. For example, imagine you dream about becoming a famous singer. Your first goal could be, for instance, singing in front of a crowd of people. How can you get there? Come up with a plan and break it into small, manageable steps, such as

- Learn how to sing.
- Join a choir or a band.
- Find a location for your first gig.
- Get people to attend your concerts.

Each of these steps is a goal on its own and can be further divided into smaller, easier-to-fulfill steps. For example, for "Learn how to sing," you can split it into the following steps:

- Find music tutors nearby.
- Book my first singing lesson.
- Schedule daily practice time.
- Get feedback.

And so on.

Even if, at some point, you need to change a part of your plan, this doesn't mean you give up on your goal entirely, only that you find an alternative way to reach it. Let's say you found a band, but your singing style didn't fit. This doesn't mean you are a bad singer or a failure, but that you have to keep searching for musicians with a style similar to yours.

Setting goals in your life provides you with direction and focus, and helps you stay motivated and find a sense of purpose for everything you do. Even something seemingly unrelated to your dream can become significant: "Setting challenging goals can increase motivation, as individuals are more likely to be engaged and invested in achieving a personally meaningful and challenging goal" (Sharma, 2023). In the same example, let's imagine you got a part-time job in a cafeteria, you may find it motivating to remember you'll use some of that paycheck to pay for your singing lessons! You'll also be more open to new opportunities: Maybe some musicians play at the cafeteria on Friday evening, and you could end up talking to them about music. Then, who knows?

It's normal to be scared, especially when we think we may fail. You know what? You will fail. But that's all part of your learning process (Maurice, 2017):

Failing you find another method that doesn't work. You get new experiences, learn, and become stronger. Failure after failure you get closer to your dream life. After some time, you realize you have no reason to quit trying, as the hardest part of the way is passed. You make findings and keep moving. (para. 21)

With enough time management and organizational skills, you'll be more prepared than ever to turn your dreams into plans, to break up big goals into manageable steps. And to live your life as you wish to live it.

As my son Ethan improved his time management skills, he found his way into college to pursue his dream of becoming a lawyer. He learned how to plan his classes and studying sessions to save commuting time, and now that he has a job in a small but promising law firm, his bosses tell him that being organized is one of the traits they value the most.

The last time I visited him, he managed to cook a delicious curry dish while answering some emails on his phone at the same time. He remembered how much I like Indian food, and he had got all the ingredients in advance to surprise me. I also noticed he's in better shape than ever because, despite his busy agenda, he had squeezed in some CrossFit training sessions a few times a week. I felt so proud of him!

Now that you're equipped with tools to better organize yourself, let's learn about one of the major adulting skills to acquire: Becoming responsible and accountable for everything you do, both in-person and online.

Chapter 6

Responsibility and Accountability— Most Times, It Is Up to You!

> In the long run, we shape our lives, and we shape ourselves. The process never ends until we die. And the choices we make are ultimately our responsibility.
>
> — Eleanor Roosevelt, former First Lady of the United States and human rights advocate.

> The price of greatness is responsibility.
>
> — Winston Churchill, renowned British Prime Minister and leader during World War II.

WHEN ALL THREE children were still living under my roof, we developed a system for them to help with age-appropriate household chores. We had a chart hanging on the kitchen wall that showed what each child was responsible for on different days of the week, and it worked out for the most part. Being the youngest, Sophia always managed to do the least—like watering the indoor plants—while Lucas and Ethan handled more tricky jobs such as loading and unloading the dishwasher, doing the laundry, or changing the sheets on their beds.

However, sometimes, this meant that children took their responsibilities *too* literally. I remember one time I found a pool of water on the floor, next to the plants. Nobody told me about it, and I think that's what made me suspicious in the first place. I went, "Okay, so who did this?" Both boys looked at each other and pointed at Sophia, who was 9 years old then. "I didn't do it on purpose, Mom! Plus, I had to water the plants, which I did! It was Ethan's turn to mop the floors, see?" Ethan, then 15, hurried to say: "Which I would have done if I hadn't been busy folding the laundry Lucas was supposed to!" To which Lucas, 13, responded, "Hey, you were going to cover for me as I did last week during your soccer practice, remember?"

I don't need to explain how a little mess escalated into a full argument between my three children, right? In the end, I got the three of them to clean the floor, and that evening, there was no TV. They were angry at each other, but in the end, the whole incident helped us further discuss domestic duties and elaborate on what being responsible and accountable meant.

I'm sure something similar has happened to you with your siblings or your friends—for example, when an assignment wasn't completed on time and it was supposed to be teamwork—as it's a common trait for children and teens to do whatever to avoid getting in trouble. It's no big deal when you're young, but the same attitude displays immaturity once you reach adulthood. That's why, in this chapter, we'll learn all about responsibility and accountability, two basic adulting skills you'll apply in every single area of your life.

Some Basic Definitions

Responsibility and accountability are words often used to describe positive traits in leadership. In conversations, more often than not, they are used as synonyms, but these are two different concepts— although closely interrelated. Let's see the meaning of each and some examples to illustrate them.

What Is Responsibility?

When we talk about responsibility, it means that something is your duty—or your job—to deal with, it is task-oriented, and it can be shared by members of a team: "Responsibility is, essentially, the duty to complete a task that someone is meant to complete" (Valladolid, 2021). Sometimes, you're assigned responsibility for one thing or another, and you don't like it, but it's just the way things work in life.

For example, if your mom asks you and your brother to tidy up the bedroom you share, you're both responsible for picking up the trash on the floor, putting the dirty clothes in the hamper, organizing the papers that lie on the desk, and making the beds. However, you and your brother could discuss splitting the task, and one of you is in charge of picking up everything that's on the floor while the other one puts everything back in its place. In any case, your mom should come home from work and find a tidy bedroom.

What Is Accountability?

As for accountability, it means that in a certain situation, a person *accepts* that given responsibility and can provide a satisfactory response to the result of events. It focuses more on the result of the task than on the task itself, and you become accountable, given that you have specific skills, competence, and experience. You are accountable when you decide to take responsibility, and you are committed either to completing it or to facing the consequences of not doing so: "[Accountability] means taking ownership to ensure responsibilities are achieved, the duty to report on tasks and events" (Valladolid, 2021).

Following the given example, let's say it was up to you to make the beds and put the clothes in the hamper. After you finish doing it, you still find a pile of papers on the desk, and your brother has gone to play video games with his friends. In any case, you know your mother won't find the bedroom as expected. Now you have two choices: You could blame your brother for not doing his part of the deal, or you could tidy up the desk yourself.

If you choose the first option, sure, you don't have to do any extra work right away, but your mother will probably be upset about the room being untidy, and your brother will get mad at you for telling on him. If you, on the other hand, decide to make yourself accountable and finish tidying up on your own, your mother will be pleased with the overall result. You could later talk to your brother and sort things out with him—maybe next time he'll be willing to cover for you, and if he doesn't, then you can talk to your mother and request not to share responsibilities with him anymore.

How to Become Accountable

Ever since you were a child, your parents, your teachers, and other adults have probably been teaching you about responsibility. Whenever your dad requests you set the table while he finishes preparing a meal, or when you get your first pet under the condition you feed them every day, or when teachers give you homework, they are making you responsible for different tasks.

However, becoming accountable isn't something that can be imposed: It's up to you to decide. Sure, when things don't go as expected, you can blame others or give excuses, but this won't help you anymore once you become an adult. Your mother may have written you a note to excuse you from skipping PE, your teacher may have allowed you to hand in a paper late, or your soccer coach may have believed you when you said you tripped and you didn't mean to kick your opponent, but that doesn't work anymore as an adult.

Sometimes, college professors will take no excuses, and you may fail the course regardless of whether you were really sick when you were absent from that exam. Your landlord may not realize or take into account that you got fired, and this month, you can't pay your rent on time. That police officer will trust their eyes, and not your excuses, for you going past the stop sign. That same lack of accountability adults may find annoying in you as a teenager will make your adult life truly hard unless you acquire the skill.

So, how can you make yourself accountable?

• **Understand what the others expect from you.** The first step in creating a habit of accountability is knowing exactly what your responsibilities are and how you are expected to act in each circumstance. With luck, your parents will have provided you with clear expectations and limits, but even if this is not the case, you can always ask. Do it calmly and not implying you want to skip any responsibility: "So the way I understand it, you expect me to arrive at nine today, right? What shall I do if the friend who's supposed to drive me home isn't ready to leave yet? Can I call you and let you know we'll be a little late? Or should I take an Uber?"

• **Deal with the fact that some rules aren't fair.** Perhaps your new boss requested you to stay an hour longer because you missed a bus and showed up 15 minutes late. Maybe your mom forgot how you washed the dishes the last four times and still asks you again instead of your lazy sister. Or it could be a teacher handing your paper back with a C- because you selected a different font size than the one they requested. You will probably dislike some of the rules people set. And guess what? This will still happen when you're an adult. The government may raise taxes, a financial institution may charge you big interest for being a few hours late on one of your payments, or the company you've been working so hard for may decide it's time for a reduction and let you go. Although in certain circumstances, you can negotiate the rules in your favor, at other times, you need to nod in acceptance... or face the consequences of not doing so.

• **Commit yourself to fulfilling your responsibilities.** Proactive accountability is about doing whatever is in your hands to make sure the tasks you are responsible for are accomplished. Imagine that you and your classmate have to handle a lab report. They were in charge of printing the file, but they forgot. Being proactively accountable means going during your lunch break to the school library and printing the report yourself to hand in when you were supposed to: "This is far better than reactive accountability, in which team members and leaders hold themselves accountable for failures without taking adequate steps to prevent them" (Sergeeva, 2021).

• **Stop giving excuses.** "It wasn't my fault!" "It was there when I got here." "I'm sorry, but here's the thing..." "You see, what happened is…" Do you usually find that adults get irritated when you explain why you didn't do as expected, even when your point is valid? Sure, unexpected things can get in the way: You were supposed to wash the car, but it's pouring outside, or you have a doctor's certificate stating that you have to spend a month on bed rest because you caught mono. But sometimes, excuses are just excuses! When, for some reason, you didn't fulfill your responsibility, it's always better to be upfront, apologize, and negotiate a new opportunity. Chances are, if you've demonstrated your accountability in the past, the consequences for an occasional mishap won't be severe.

• **Don't blame others.** Just like giving excuses doesn't build trust or make you accountable, arguing that something was someone else's fault doesn't help you either. Sure, there is such a thing as shared responsibility, and sometimes other people will fail you. It's not up to you to make *them* accountable. All you can do is accept your part and consider whether in the future you'll choose to share your responsibility with some other person, or at least state things clearly. For example, if your roommate didn't pay the electricity bill as they were expected to, you pay them instead to keep the company from cutting the service, but you may consider asking them to find a new place to live if the situation keeps happening.

• **Accept the consequences of your actions.** Part of being accountable is maturely accepting the consequences of failing to fulfill a task. Being accountable means that you're responsible. This can mean apologizing to an angry customer when one of your employees responds inappropriately, paying the higher interest to your loan company if you forgot to submit the check on the payment day, or accepting that your parents ground you because you failed a course. Accepting the blame is reactive accountability, although it isn't as effective as being proactively accountable.

Developing Your Decision-Making Skills

A major part of becoming accountable is being able to make a decision when given two or more choices, as well as answering for those decisions that you made (Sergeeva, 2021). But decision-making isn't just important for being accountable: It's the most important aspect of transitioning into adulthood!

The term "adulting" is frequently used in a derogatory way: "Adulting is the assumption of tasks, responsibilities, and behaviors traditionally associated with normal grown-up life, along with the implication that the individual in question does not particularly identify as an adult and that acting as one does not come naturally" (Wigmore, 2017). In social media, the word is often used to label millennials and their lack of skills for things previous generations were used to doing (such as sacrificing their social life for putting in long extra hours at work, getting into debt buying their first house, or home cooking), without acknowledging that the world young people live today has little to do with the one former generations grew up in.

So, at this point, I want to state clearly what I mean by being an adult. It's not about sacrificing your whole work/life balance, as young people today are more aware of the importance of mental health and gratification that goes beyond making money; it's not about embracing old traditions without questioning them or doing the same things your parents did when they were your age; and it's not about getting married and having kids, since we know now that these are life *choices*, not impositions.

Instead, I believe the core of becoming an adult is going from others making the decision and you following or being influenced by others and having others take responsibility, to following your lead and making your own decisions as you develop your value system, having to own the corresponding responsibility and consequences.

In other words, what I mean is that you can live with your parents and still be an adult, you can decide you don't want to buy a house and instead, travel six months a year, or you can change jobs as many times you want in search of your dream career.

But whatever it is you decide, you have to become accountable for those decisions. Life shouldn't be something that just *happens* to you, but rather something you consciously *build* by the choices you make. In this way, you won't find yourself complaining about life being "unfair," because life is something you create as you learn to navigate the possibilities that come as years go by. That's why learning how to make decisions is, by far, a more important adulting skill than home cooking or opening a number of bank accounts.

Some young people feel stuck in their teenage years or seem unable to mature because they are paralyzed when facing a decision. The thing is, *not* doing anything about something is still choosing. In other words, if you decide, for example, to live with your parents way into your 20s, let it be a conscious choice from your side and not something you're simply stuck to. Take responsibility for your choice by being an adult at home and not relying on your parents for household tasks or giving you money anytime you need to go out or get a new jacket. To be a mature adult, that sense of responsibility should expand from the individual to the family, social community, and beyond, as self-awareness and self-conviction grow stronger, allowing for deeper understanding and unwavering beliefs.

How to Make the Right Decisions

What could stop you from effective decision-making? These are some factors to consider, and you can't make a conscious, well-informed decision if you don't take them into account.

• **Get all the vital information.** If you don't fully understand a situation, you're likely to make a mistake. For example, you may decide you don't want to start college when you finish high school, and you'd rather take a sabbatical year. But maybe you're not aware that it would be more difficult to obtain a loan the older you are. Explore the consequences of your decisions before jumping into one.

• **Identify the problem.** Maybe you don't want to stay in a job because your boss gives you a hard time whenever you show up late, but are you sure your boss is the problem? Unless you do something to change your habits, being late is likely to be an issue in any job you get in the future: "Be clear that your decision addresses a root cause, not just a symptom" (*How to make decisions*, n.d.).

• **Consider the potential risks.** When facing a decision, sometimes we only take a look at the positive consequences but fail to address the negative ones. Sure, living with your parents while in college may save you some money in rent, but you'll resign your privacy and independence. Are you sure that's a price you're willing to pay?

• **Communicate**. Some of your decisions don't only involve you. Make sure you discuss them with other people affected by them. For example, if you are planning on moving out of an apartment you share with a roommate, make sure you tell them in advance so they can start looking for another person to share rent with.

Decision-making is an art of selection, and it has very much to do with our core beliefs and identity. Every choice we intentionally make builds a life that closes off countless others. This challenge extends beyond simply weighing two or more equally difficult options, each with its own set of sacrifices. Every decision is testament to how far into the future of possibilities we are wise enough to discern and accept, all the while guided by our convictions, an understanding of how the world operates, and an awareness of the potential prices that may need to be paid in time to come. There is no definitive right or wrong decision, since all decisions are somewhat right, and at the same time somewhat wrong. It all boils down to our values, and acceptance. They are the litmus test of whether we can truly live with our decisions, striving to keep regrets to the minimum.

Let Your Values Guide You

During our teenage years, we're more aware than ever of the way others look at us. We experience peer pressure, and our choices and decisions are likely to be influenced by what others tell us. Sometimes, even after growing up, people hold on to this dependence:

"Too often in life, we either do things because everyone else seems to be doing them, or because, like an idle sailboat bobbing about in the open sea, we somehow drift into them" (Itani, 2021).

When my son Ethan told his father and me that he had refused a job offer last year, at first, we were concerned. Joining a reputable commercial law firm seemed like an opportunity too good to waste! Why would he let it pass, knowing that it may cost him a position others in his place would pay for?

But becoming a self-conscious, responsible adult means, among other things, letting your inner values guide you in your decisions instead of relying on external pressure. Ethan told us that he'd rather opt for a small firm that allowed him to work on civil rights law than spend so much time and energy in business law. He had decided to follow his passion, even if it meant making less money. After he put it this way, his father and I supported his decision. Even if you make a mistake, it's better to do so believing you were doing the right thing than being pressured by others. That's why figuring out what matters the most to you in life and, overall, what kind of person you want to become is the best way to make decisions.

On the other hand, living a life just to fulfill external expectations may leave you feeling empty and lost, even if your life looks great to everyone around you. For example, if you discover your value is curiosity and learning, what's the point of earning good money through a repetitive job if you are not happy with your daily life? Soon, you'll find yourself unmotivated and your actions meaningless. Okay, for some people, making money is the definition of success, but are you sure it is yours? "When you don't set your own values, you will end up losing yourself in the values of other people. Your identity, self-worth, and the way you lead your life will then become totally contingent upon the value system of others" (Itani, 2021).

To find out what your core values are, begin by asking yourself a question: *What matters most to me?* As you discover your values, make a list and define them. For example, if one of your values is health, consider both physical, emotional, and mental health. Keep your core values in sight and let them guide you whenever you need to make any important decisions. For example, for my son Ethan, helping people was a personal value that guided him more than becoming wealthy. Similarly, knowing health is one of your values, put it in the first place when you consider a job offer.

Finally, no one can tell you what your core values are, it's up to you to discover them and then, let them guide you. They will become the compass to walk you through life, a life that's true to you and feels authentic, built by you, and not simply occurring: "Intentional living is about scripting your personal values and then actively living your daily life in alignment with those values" (Itani, 2021).

The Thing About Procrastination

Do you find it hard to get motivated? Do you sometimes feel lost when facing a challenging task, and you don't even know where to start? Do you find your duties long, tedious, or boring? Or are you frequently overwhelmed with decision-making up to the point in which you are paralyzed?

Sometimes you know what needs to be done, or what the best decision to make is; however, you take a long time to start working on it. That act of delaying tasks until the last possible minute or even past their deadline is known as procrastination, and almost all of us experience it from time to time. Sure, the instant gratification you get from spending five more minutes scrolling through your phone or sending a meme to your best friend is more rewarding than folding laundry, doing your homework, or paying your bills, but it doesn't do anything else for you.

The problem begins when procrastination becomes the norm rather than the exception. If you constantly struggle to make decisions or to start necessary tasks, you may be suffering from chronic procrastination. You are not the only one: A 2007 study found out 80% to 95% of U.S. college students procrastinate when they need to complete assignments, and 1 in every 5 adults is a chronic procrastinator (Cherry, 2022a).

Types of Procrastination

While procrastination can be a symptom of mental conditions such as depression, obsessive-compulsive disorder (OCD), or attention deficit hyperactivity disorder (ADHD), you could also suffer from procrastination as a result of some personality traits. That's why, to stop procrastinating, it's good to figure out why you do it in the first place.

First of all, consider whether you're a passive or an active procrastinator: Do you make excuses and find yourself avoiding a specific chore, forgetting about it, or finding yourself busy with something else until you hate yourself because you're running out of time? Or do you *deliberately* delay the start of a project because you feel you work better under pressure?

In the first case, you're more likely to be negatively affected: Passive procrastination—also called traditional or avoidant—is likely to cause anxiety, poor self-esteem, and bad results. On the other hand, active procrastination is, for some people, an adaptive mechanism that is less likely to interfere with their daily lives (Shatz, n.d.). For example, you may find you can finish your presentation when preparing it the night before, even if you are given a week. The problem is when you miscalculate; for example, if you underestimate how long it will take you to complete it.

Other experts classify types of procrastinators according to how they feel and behave. According to psychologist Jayson Moran, some people procrastinate because they experience anxiety in some form (Moran, 2022):

• A worrier avoids completing a task because they feel they may fail at doing it.

• A perfectionist believes a task that isn't perfect isn't worth doing it.

• An over-doer tends to feel overwhelmed because they commit to multiple tasks and haven't learned to prioritize them.

Moran also distinguishes some types of procrastinators motivated by boredom or frustration:

• A crisis-maker believes they perform better under pressure (although they aren't always right!).

• A dreamer keeps expecting "inspiration" and postponing tasks if they don't feel motivated enough.

• Finally, a defier refuses to spend time and energy doing something only "because they're supposed to."

How to Stop Procrastinating

While procrastination, in some cases and to some degree, can become part of a person's lifestyle, it may become a serious issue once it begins affecting different areas in your life, such as your work, your finances, your studies, your health, or your relationships. If this is your case, you may wonder how you can stop procrastinating and get in control of your life. Depending on which feelings and beliefs trigger your procrastination, you may find these suggestions useful:

• **Break the task down.** If you find complex tasks overwhelming up to the point you don't even start doing them in the first place, break them into smaller, more manageable tasks. Sure, writing an admission letter to college sounds like a lot. How about writing the opening paragraph? You'll be able to complete it shortly, and you'll feel more motivated to take the next step.

• **Set realistic deadlines for each step.** Perhaps you feel motivated under pressure, but the results of rushed work will never be as satisfactory as the ones from something carefully planned and developed. So, you want to finish your dissertation the night before? It's up to you, but commit yourself to finishing research two weeks before, writing the draft a week later, and so on.

• **Keep your distractions away.** Once you know how you usually procrastinate, remove anything distracting. For example, if you have to work on your paper, turn off the TV and put away your phone. Close any unnecessary tabs on your computer, and commit yourself to working for a limited yet uninterrupted period. Also, be aware of internal procrastination: "You might say to yourself, 'I will do these other little things first and then get to the important task.' However, these other 'little things' often contribute to the cycle of procrastination" (Low, 2023).

• **Use social pressure the right way.** Telling your friends and family about your project is a good way for them to keep you accountable. Let your roommate know you'll be calling the plumber this afternoon. Or tell your dad about how you joined the gym, and you are starting your training today.

• **Make boring tasks fun.** Let's accept that some tasks will always be boring, and you'll never feel inspired or motivated to complete them! And still, this doesn't mean you can't avoid them forever. Turn them into something more exciting instead: Do you have to wash the dishes? Play music while you do so, or challenge yourself to complete the task in less time than it took you yesterday.

Adulting Online: Watch Out for Your Digital Footprint

Before we move on to our next chapter, let's take some time to consider responsibility and accountability in the digital world. What does it mean to be an adult online? While you may believe at first that whatever you do on social media isn't as important as how you act in other areas of your life, the world we live in is also digital. Therefore, you must act responsibly online as well, and be accountable for your actions: Mainly, what you publish, how you publish it, how you answer to people, and so on.

Leaving Trace

Perhaps you've heard of the concept of "digital footprint," or digital shadow. It refers to the trail of data that comes as a result of all your online activity: Whenever you send an email, post on social media, follow somebody, subscribe to a newsletter, shop online, comment on some news, or even do a search, part of that information remains. People may access it, and their purposes aren't always harmless.

An estimated 64% of the world population is an internet user, which means there are about 5.16 billion unique digital footprints. And we use the internet, like, *a lot*: "The average adult willingly shares 276 posts on Instagram, 170 on Facebook, and 141 tweets every year, amounting to an active digital footprint containing 9,828 photos, 10,811 social media posts, and 126 email addresses throughout a lifetime" (Bizga, 2023). You may think you're safe because you use a nickname instead of your real name, but the truth is more than half of the online community has over a dozen data points exposed online, and 16% of them have more than 50 instances of personal information available: "This includes home addresses, URLs linking to social media platforms, job titles and workplaces, names, usernames, email addresses, and phone numbers" (Bizga, 2023). So, the first thing to take into account is that you are not anonymous when you do something online.

Secondly, consider that you lose control of everything you leave in your digital footprint, as most of the content can't easily be deleted. You are building a reputation online that may even remain after you are dead: Social media accounts—such as Facebook, Instagram, or Twitter—can't be easily deactivated unless you are 18 or older and you designate a legacy contact, who is someone you trust and authorize to erase your data. For the deceased, data protection legislation no longer applies (Benson, 2022):

In the US, there are currently no laws that specifically extend to "post-mortem privacy" protection. Most terms and services for things like social media accounts set up licenses and rights between you and the company, which may fall to the company if you die. (para. 31)

Imagine if your voice and images are then used commercially to build AI narrators and actors. Even in death, you may still be working virtually in advertising or as an AI service! If I were to let my imagination run further, I envision a world where AI algorithms and generative technologies converge. They create human images and voices based on the traits of our deceased family and relatives, even those unknown to us. The end result is an avatar that we feel oddly familiar with, biologically close to and that we inherently trust. The question is, would future advertisers capitalize on this unregulated novel approach? Would they sell us hyper-personalized campaigns that resonate on an unprecedented level?

Consequences of Your Digital Footprint

Most search engines and social media platforms collect your personal data to personalize your online experience. You may have noticed how, for instance, after buying a t-shirt online, your screen becomes full of ads for sportswear. Or, after searching for information about a specific topic—for example, a book for your literature class—you receive suggestions for writers and publishers. If a commercial digital footprint were all that existed, it wouldn't be so terrible.

But others can access your data as well. In the best-case scenario, it may be a potential employer, a college, or a security company checking your online reputation. That embarrassing photo where one of your friends tagged you or that hateful comment you posted without thinking too much may cost you a job in the future: "The opinions you share on message boards, social media, or news websites can significantly impact your reputation and your credibility" (*What is a digital footprint*, n.d.).

In the worst possible case, your digital footprint may turn you into the victim of fraud, blackmail, scams, or even identity theft. Think about everything people do online, from opening bank accounts to buying cryptocurrency, from creating a fake dating app to cheat on their spouses to publishing intimate pictures. Not taking care of your digital footprint may potentially cause you embarrassment, a damaged reputation, and leave you in complete vulnerability.

Protecting Yourself Online

So, how can you be mindful of your digital footprint and prevent it from backfiring? First, you have some tools provided by technology, such as password managers (to help you generate and periodically change all of your passwords), firewalls, virtual private networks (VPN), etc. But some of the most essential precautions refer to the way you behave online:

• **Think before you post anything:** Instead of sending pic after pic or trolling someone with a sarcastic remark, take some time to consider the potential consequences of publishing that content online. Everything you publish says more about yourself than about the other person: "Create a positive digital footprint by posting only those things that contribute to the image of you that you want others to see" (Kaspersky, 2021).

• **Be extra careful when using public Wi-Fi:** Never disclose personal data (such as your Social Security number, medical information, or credit card number) on a public network. You never know who could be monitoring your activity.

• **Check your digital footprint on a search engine:** You can Google yourself to see the amount of information currently available to anyone. Whenever you notice something that shows you negatively, you should contact the website and ask for that data to be removed. The same applies to websites that display personal information. Set up a Google Alert with your name so you can keep up-to-date with new data that may become available in the future.

• **Check your privacy settings:** Whenever you open an account on social media, review the settings so you only allow access to people you're comfortable with.

• **Don't keep old accounts active:** Reduce your digital footprint by deleting old email accounts or social media.

We've discussed some ways to become a responsible and accountable adult, both in-person and online: Being able to provide an answer when you are expected, making informed decisions, not procrastinating, and keeping an eye on your reputation. All of these are basic steps for joining the workforce, which will be the topic of the following chapter.

Chapter 7

Finding a Job—Fit Yourself for the Workforce

> Your work is going to fill a large part of your life, and the only way to be truly satisfied is to do what you believe is great work.
>
> — Steve Jobs, co-founder of Apple Inc.

WORKING, and working *hard*, is one of the first premises any teen has about what being an adult means. Maybe this is because you grow up hearing us folks complaining about how tired we are, how you should appreciate the food on the table, or how expensive living gets. Maybe you hear less about how much fun we can have in our job, or how great it feels to contribute to society with it.

Sure, there's that saying—attributed either to a Chinese philosopher who lived 2,500 years ago or to a current U.S. singer, depending on your source (McCallum, 2016)—that states that if you choose to do something you love for a living, then you won't need to work a single day of your life—that sounds great except it is not true. You'll still work, and although you will enjoy it *most* of the time, it's plain impossible to enjoy anything at all times, so the saying creates false expectations, to say the least.

As in other aspects of adult life, the key is finding a balance.

You'll work. You'll work hard sometimes. You'll meet great people and others who are not as good. You'll make mistakes. You'll learn. And you can enjoy your work most of the time if you choose wisely and learn from those mistakes.

We've already talked about how small part-time gigs can help you save money in Chapter 4, even while you're still in middle school. This chapter will deal with tips on joining the workforce as an adult and how to put yourself out there and impress the world. With patience and perseverance, you'll land a job that gives you satisfaction and fulfillment besides money.

Choosing a Career, Considerations

A career is more than just a gig walking your neighbor's dog or buying and selling collectibles for a profit, as it is the sum of your professional journey. If you consider that any average person spends approximately one-third of their life working, you shouldn't be surprised that so many of us wish to find a career that is a good fit: "Choosing a career first means learning as much as you can about yourself, your goals, and the larger context of work" (*How to choose a career*, 2023).

What to Do When Undecided

When you are in high school, you literally have thousands of career options ahead. And while you can change your career during your lifetime—as many people do—now that you are in your late teens or early 20s, you need to focus on finding a path that suits your interests, your needs, and your motivations.

For some young people, the path seems to be clear. For example, Ethan's girlfriend, Joanne, told me she knew she was going to be a veterinarian ever since she was 5, and now that she's about to graduate, she's as certain as always of her desire. For most teens, there's usually a period of confusion or indecision when it comes to choosing a career path. If this is your case, here are some steps to follow:

1. Learn about yourself: Know about your skills, your aptitudes, your interests, and your personality type. You can use self-assessment tools and career tests to help you limit your options and have approximate ideas of what would make a good career fit. While you can always go to a counselor to help you navigate the process, you'll also find many free tools online you can begin to explore right away. Career coach Kyle Elliott suggests you also ask people around you: "Ask friends, family members, and other people you trust what roles they could envision you doing for a living. You can also inquire as to the companies they could see you working at" (Ingram, 2022).

2. List possible careers: After taking several tests, write down a list of those careers that appear more than once among your test results—chances are you'll still have a bunch of them, as career tests provide you with a variety of options. Then, include in your list any occupation that appeared among the results and caught your interest. Finally, include options that you know little about: Who knows? Maybe there's a great professional path ahead you've never even considered, but you'd be great at it. There you go: The careers on your list are options for you to further research. By now, instead of thousands, you may have limited your options to 10–20.

3. Find out more about your choices: Now it's time to get basic information about the careers on your list. Dawn Rosenberg McKay (2022), from *The Balance*, suggests you "Find job descriptions and educational, training, and licensing requirements in published sources. Learn about advancement opportunities. Use government-produced labor market information to get data about earnings and job outlook." This will help you narrow your list further until you only have a handful of choices.

4. Interview experts: For that short list you've come up with, try to contact people who work in each field. For example, when my son Ethan was doing this exercise, he spoke to a friend of mine who is a lawyer, his counselor from high school who is also a licensed psychologist, and because he didn't know any journalist in person, he contacted a few of them on LinkedIn who were willing to answer his questions. This way, he learned more about what the day-to-day of those professions really were. It helped him make up his mind and follow a career in law, something that wasn't his first choice when he started his research.

Life Balance or the Concept of Ikigai

After you've decided upon a career, you'll be able to set up a plan, including what to study, for how long, where, and which kind of jobs you can apply to that will help you reach your professional goals. Sources like the U.S. Bureau of Labor Statistics may help you spot the fastest-growing industries in which you'll find more job and salary opportunities.

However, keep in mind what we discussed in the previous chapter about your core values: While for some people, making money is their basic definition of success, perhaps you want freedom more than anything or spending time with your future family instead. According to Elliot, "If you want to spend more time with your children, for instance, ask yourself which option would move you closer to this goal" (Ingram, 2022).

There's a Japanese word that means life and realization of hope and expectations: *Ikigai* is more than just a word, it's a concept that combines what you love, what you do for money, what the world needs, and what you're good at. It represents life balance (Annisa, 2021). It's not easy, and some people spend a lot of their lifetime in that search or simply resign themselves to an aspect of it. For example

• The successful auditioner who is great at their job and brings home a juicy paycheck, but in their little free time still dreams about getting on a stage.

• The environmental activist who dedicates a lot of their time and energy to their cause, but although already in their mid-30s, hasn't managed to move out of their parents' home.

• The stay-at-home parent who enjoys spending time with their children and seeing them grow up but sometimes misses being in control of their own money and not depending on their partner for a living.

• The creative who has a lot of fun designing a social media campaign and seeing it thrive but secretly doesn't truly believe the product or service they are selling makes the world any better.

Doing something you love and helping the world can be your mission, but maybe it won't pay the bills. Doing something you're good at and getting paid for it may be your profession, but it leaves you feeling empty. On the contrary, when you manage to find something that brings you satisfaction, excitement, comfort, and delight at the same time, you'll be certain that you've found your sense of purpose or *Ikigai*. But just the fact that you're considering the search and that you do your best to be as close to a bigger life purpose will increase your chances of walking a happier, more successful, and overall fulfilling professional path.

Creating an Impressive Resume

A resume is the first way your potential employer can learn about you, your skills, and your experience, and help them find out whether you'll be suitable for a certain job. By creating an easy-to-read, strong resume that summarizes your best traits, you maximize your chances of landing in a great position that will help you move forward in your career.

But with so many other candidates available, how can you make sure your resume stands out? Here are some tips for writing and submitting an effective resume:

• **Put the relevant information first.** Highlight your relevant skills and experience. If you don't have any work history directly related to that job search, you can present other experiences—such as school projects—creatively: "Draw on the skills you used and how your contributions benefited the organization or project" (Caramela, 2023).

• **Keep it short and relevant.** You may have an impressive list of courses, extracurricular activities, exams, or maybe previous experience you feel you should list, but employers won't waste time reading more than one page. So, make sure you only include the information that's relevant to the job you're applying for. Sure, you can save a big resume file on your computer but pay attention to each job posting and tailor your resume to fit every specific search: "As you apply for different jobs, study each job description for keywords that show what the employer is looking for in an ideal candidate. Include those keywords in your resume where relevant" (Northup, 2023).

• **Be objective:** Avoid using words such as "professional," "responsible," or "successful." It's better to provide numbers to quantify your success: "Metrics can highlight your achievements and give the hiring manager or recruiter a clear sense of how you impacted your previous place of employment" (Caramela, 2023). Therefore, instead of presenting yourself as "a great student," it's better to submit your average grades.

• **Use a good template.** Employers value originality, so stay away from basic Microsoft Office templates, or at least personalize them. You can find more attractive templates available online, such as in Canva. In any case, you need to find a balance between originality and professionalism. Use headings and subheadings for clarity, and try to restrain your choices of fonts to traditional ones such as Arial, Times New Roman, or Helvetica.

• **Proofread.** Nothing is less appealing to a potential employer than seeing typos or misspelled words in a resume. Make sure you run software such as Grammarly to keep your resume well-written. Also, check for inconsistencies in formatting, as they show a lack of technical skills or little attention to detail: "Your resume is your first—and often only—chance to impress a potential employer, and you should treat it as such" (Caramela, 2023).

Put Yourself Out There!

Once you decide to go job hunting, something you have to do other than writing your resume is letting people know you're looking for a job. Tell anyone since you never know who may have heard about a possible opportunity: Your parents, your teachers and professors, your friends, people at your gym, even your neighbors. Ask them if you can send them your resume in case they think of something.

Your contact network may not know of a job for you, but they can help you in other ways, mostly by becoming a reference. This is especially significant if you have no solid work experience, as your potential employer may request someone to speak to about your qualities. A letter from a college professor or a recommendation from someone in the same field you're trying to start your career in may do wonders for your job search.

Forget about the image you may have seen in pictures of the unemployed person with a newspaper folded under their armpit. Nowadays, the internet is your primary source for any job hunt. Check job postings online every day and set alerts for keywords that interest you. And if you haven't done it so far, create a profile on LinkedIn: With over 130 million users in the US alone and present in over 200 countries, it's the top professional social networking site, used by 87% of recruiters when they are searching for the perfect candidate (Suder, 2016).

What works great about this platform is that it allows you to combine both your resume and your network. However, to stand out, you need to make the most out of it and not just open an account and fill it with data. Even if you're not actively job-hunting, keeping your profile complete and up-to-date is always a good idea so potential recruiters can spot you online. Here are some tips for making the best out of LinkedIn:

• **Create a profile as a personal brand.** While a resume should be concise, LinkedIn allows you to expand, highlight your qualities, and personalize your profile. You're not just applying for a job; you're selling your services. Make sure you include relevant keywords you may find in job descriptions similar to the one you're looking for.

• **Make sure you complete your profile.** Don't leave blank spaces, and make sure you include a profile picture so the search algorithm will help you stand out: "You're far more likely to show up in search results with a complete profile. LinkedIn assigns different strengths to profiles based on their completeness" (Borsellino, 2021).

- **Choose your headline wisely.** Your job title or your degree isn't enough. Instead of writing *Johanna Smith—Journalist*, highlight your best traits and specific skills that may set you apart: *Johanna Smith. Graphic journalist specializing in photography and infographics.*

- **Exchange recommendations.** After exporting your contacts from Google, make sure some of your contacts can provide a robust and relevant recommendation. You should give one in return to your colleagues to help them out on their job searches as well. You can also increase your contact network by looking for alumni of your same college or university (Suder, 2016).

- **Be an active user.** Besides regularly updating your profile, make sure you post updates, articles you write, videos, and so on. Get involved in professional groups, and follow companies that interest you. According to career consultant Jordan Hallow, after a year of actively contacting other users, commenting on their posts, and writing content, his followers increased by 600%, and his profile views an astounding 1000% (Borsellino, 2021).

Preparing for an Interview

So, once you've written your resume, activated your network, and contacted a few companies, things have worked out, and you have an interview. This is the moment to show the recruiter you're the right person for the position and highlight all the skills and accomplishments you've presented in your online profile.

At the same time, think of the interview as your chance to find out whether this job is suitable for you. Sometimes, you may perceive that it's not quite what you were looking for. One time, my son Ethan decided to opt out of a job after the recruiter told him how they expected "flexibility" and "full commitment," which, in other words, meant he was expected to do overtime, answer emails on weekends, and pretty much devote himself to a job that didn't offer growth opportunities or a great working environment in return.

Before Attending the Interview

On the days before your interview, make sure you fully understand the job description you're interviewing for. Be suspect of vague descriptions or promises of easy money, as they are usually scams such as pyramid schemes and not legit job offers. A proper job description should include a job title, duties and tasks, and skills required (Half, 2016). Besides, from the description, you can get ideas about the possible questions you may need to answer during the interview so you can be prepared to answer them.

Secondly, research the company and the position. You need to attend the interview knowing about the product or service they offer, the company culture, their main competitors, and, if possible, the executive team. You can find out a lot by checking the profiles of people who are currently working for them. Knowing about the company will help you come up with specific questions you can—and should—ask during your interview that will show both interest as well as professionalism.

Last but not least, make sure you get to the interview on time, if possible, arriving 15 minutes earlier. Check out traffic reports and come up with more than one choice of commuting. Go to bed early the night before and put out your clothes in advance. And bring a few printed copies of your resume, even if they tell you it's not necessary.

During the Interview

You only have one chance to create a first impression, so make sure you seize this unique opportunity. Smiling, making eye contact, and giving a strong handshake go a long way! Take mental notes of the name and title of the interviewer, and remember the details you included in your resume as well. Pay special attention to your body language during the interview: Avoid wiggling your fingers or tapping your feet, sit still, and keep your hands in sight.

Most interviews have common questions you should be prepared to answer. Here are some of them:

- **Tell me about yourself.** You don't want to memorize your resume. It's better to tell an engaging story to highlight some of the traits that make you eligible for this particular position. For example, "After I finished high school, I decided to spend six months studying abroad. This helped me gain a wide understanding of diverse cultures."

- **Why do you want to work for us?** Avoid vague responses such as "It's a great opportunity," and don't mention money at this point. If you've done your research, you'll be able to provide your recruiter with solid, specific reasons why you believe in this particular company.

- **What kind of work environment do you feel most comfortable in?** This is another one of the questions where your research will pay off. "Your preferred environment should closely align to the company's workplace culture (and if it doesn't, it may not be the right fit for you)" (Oliver, 2021). The same applies to whether you prefer independence or teamwork.

- **What are your salary expectations?** Always have a range of numbers in mind when you come to the interview. Of course, you may be open to negotiations, but the recruiter wants to know if your expectations match their current budget. You can get an estimate on the current industry rates by asking people in your LinkedIn community or by checking websites such as Fishbowl or Glassdoor that offer salary information.

- **Can you tell me about your flaws/one time you experienced failure?** This is, together with the year gap or how to handle pressure, one of the most awkward questions you may bump into. You don't want to look as if you memorized the answer, so it's better to ask for a moment to think about it. Then, you can tell a story about how you learned a lesson or what you're doing or planning to do to overcome something you could consider a flaw: "I tend to take more than I can handle, but in my last job, I had a great project leader who helped me learn to delegate and prioritize tasks."

Before you leave, make sure you ask the interviewer the questions you prepared in advance. For instance, you can ask about a typical day in the job position, what your main responsibilities will be, or if they can show you examples of projects you are expected to work on. You can take notes on their answers, as this will show your commitment. Of course, make sure you ask any other questions that may arise during the interview.

After the Interview

Finally, it's time to follow up with the employer. You can do it by sending them an email, mentioning your name, the date and time of the interview, and the job position you're applying to. Then, "note the company's name as well as a conversation point and/or goal that seemed especially important to the person you spoke with. Connect that point to your experience and interests" (Keiling, 2023). Thank them for the opportunity, and remind them you're looking forward to hearing from them and answering any other questions they may have.

Dressing for Work

One of the keys to a good first impression is dressing professionally. Although the dress code of a specific workplace may vary—from a business professional or business casual in typical traditional work environments to a casual or smart-casual code in modern startups or creative positions—it's better to be safe than sorry by dressing conservatively when going to your interviews.

Dressing professionally not only helps you craft a solid image, but it also boosts your self-confidence, communicates your respect toward the work position, and enhances your credibility. For example, you can opt for a dark jacket with matching pants, if possible, a shirt and a tie, and dress shoes if you're a man, and a business suit with a skirt find blazer, a long-sleeve blouse, and low high-heel shoes if you're a woman.

It's always better to dress a little too formally than to show up more informally than expected. Later, if your employer mentions the dress code is not as strict, you can always choose a more casual outfit. However, it's still advisable to stay out of your everyday clothes such as jeans, tank tops, flip-flops, sneakers, miniskirts, over-sized or too-tight clothing, or too-large pieces of jewelry.

Make sure the clothes you choose fit you perfectly, that they are clean and ironed, that every button is in its right place, and that the colors aren't flashy. Also, polish your shoes. Don't just pay attention to your attire: If you wear perfume or cologne, only choose a light scent; style your hair and make sure your nails are trim and neat, and if you have piercings or tattoos, try to keep them out of sight. In a few words, "Always consider what message your outfit is sending before wearing it" (*How to dress professional*, 2021).

What about video calls and interviews? In general, try to keep it professional but simple. Should you wear formal attire at all? As it happens with job interviews, it's always better to overdo than to be the sloppy one: "It's a little awkward to be the only one in a button-up on a video call of people in t-shirts, but it's much worse to show up to a video call in an overly casual top when others are wearing suits" (*What should I wear,* 2023). It's up to you to wear your "Zoom pants" and only dress up from the waist up, but in case you get up to grab some water or get your notes, be mindful of the camera!

With all these tips and tricks, you're ready to find yourself a great job. Our next chapter will be about how to act professionally once you are in your new position.

Chapter 8

Keeping a Job—Improving Your Workplace Skills

 Excellence is not a skill. It's an attitude.

— Ralph Marston, motivational writer and author of
"The Daily Motivator".

WHEN MY SON Lucas turned 16, he started his first home business, helping senior citizens install computers and apps on their phones. It was a huge success! Thanks to word-of-mouth, Lucas always had some work to do: What their clients found a technological nightmare, my son managed to solve in seconds.

However, things didn't work out so great when, in an attempt to make his business grow, he included a couple of his friends and started passing on some of his potential clients. Although they were great kids, people started to complain about their "attitude problems," their vocabulary, and their overall general appearance. Lucas had to apologize on their behalf, and ever since, he decided to work by himself, which also created tension with his friends!

Many teens and young people find themselves jumping from job to job, not knowing what went wrong in the first place. Even if you manage to avoid getting yourself fired, without the proper attitude at work, you may feel uncomfortable and cause that same feeling in people around you. Other times, you may get frustrated because all of your hard work isn't noticeable. In this chapter, we'll discuss how you should interact with your coworkers and superiors, how to make yourself stand out, and what the best ways to get a promotion are, among other topics.

Work Etiquette and Attitude at Work

No matter how casual your job may seem, you should always behave professionally. Whether you're serving tables at a diner or closing million-dollar deals with wealthy clients, your work attitude should always be the same. For example, standing up, making eye contact, and introducing yourself by your full name during the handshake are the best ways to create a strong, professional first impression.

One basic first rule is to arrive at your workplace on time and, if possible, arrive earlier. This shows you are fully committed: "Consistently being punctual shows that you value the time of others in your work environment" (Palmquist, 2023). Sure, you may have an emergency one day, but it should be a *real* emergency, and you should always notify your superiors that you'll be late. You also want to look alert, as sleepiness or being distracted (for example, by looking at your phone screen) always looks bad in any workplace.

How you treat others speaks a lot about you. Learn people's names and try to remember them. Save their business cards and their contact information. Always be respectful, no matter the hierarchy of the person you're talking to: Both the CEO and the receptionist are two human beings doing their job, and they both deserve respect. Avoid gossiping, criticizing others, or making personal remarks. Give credit to others when it's due, and avoid interrupting people during conversations: "Listening actively and attentively to others is an important aspect of good office etiquette" (Mishra, 2023).

Of course, conflict is an inevitable aspect of work. In the case of my son's friends, one of them lost their patience when explaining for the seventh time to a person with a hearing aid how to turn off the notifications on their phone. Don't do that with potential customers or with your coworkers: "Avoid losing your temper or getting into arguments with others. Instead, approach the situation calmly and seek to find a resolution" (Mishra, 2023).

Finally, etiquette also refers to your workspace. Pick up after yourself and make sure your cubicle or desk is tidy. While it's okay to display a couple of personal touches—such as family photos—you don't want your workspace to feel cluttered. And always respect other people's space as you wish them to respect yours.

Online Etiquette

Remember that work etiquette extends to virtuality as well. For example, always proofread your emails, making sure there are no spellings or typos, that you've completed the subject box with a relevant topic, and that you've selected the right recipient: "Pay attention when typing a name from your address book on the email's 'To' line. It is easy to select the wrong name, which you really don't want to do" (Smith, 2015).

Always be prompt in answering your emails and your calls: "To practice proper email etiquette, respond to all messages within 24 hours. If you need more time to find information or make a decision, communicate with the sender so they know you're working on the reply" (Palmquist, 2023). Avoid using work email for personal communications, and most importantly, never write in an email something that you wouldn't say to a person's face.

When it comes to working online, video calls, or Zoom meetings, there's an unwritten list of wanted and unwanted behaviors that have gained considerable importance, especially since the COVID-19 pandemic. Some of these rules are translations from the traditional in-office work etiquette, such as never arriving late to a meeting—which in this case means don't connect late—or the same as keeping your desk tidy in your office, choose a professional background for your call. Some others are more specific and may depend on whether you are the host of the meeting or just an attendant. Let's see some examples.

Any participant should familiarize themselves with the

commands and check their video and audio devices before the meeting starts. If you are the host, your camera should always be on, and you should introduce yourself as soon as the meeting starts. If you are an attendant, it's okay to leave your camera off, but certainly, it isn't the better choice because it reduces the human interaction during the meeting: "Your co-participants will not be able to read your body language, and you won't be able to provide additional context to your arguments with gestures" (James, 2022).

And speaking about body language, given that video calls don't give as much room to taking turns speaking as in natural conversations, properly requesting to speak is also a must if you don't want to spend half of the meeting interrupting each other. Unlike the camera, keeping your mic off is polite, professional, and recommended: "If you're at home, being on mute can prevent barking dogs, background noise, or your children playing from distracting other people in the meeting" (Chen, 2022). However, once it's your turn to speak, make sure you connect the mic again before you start, as not doing so may look unprofessional and slow down the meeting.

Another important detail is being fully present in the call, which means you shouldn't be opening and checking out other tabs in your browser. You may think nobody realizes, but you'll miss important details, and sometimes, people can tell from your eye movements that you're multitasking. While it's okay to have a glass of water and take a sip now and then, if you're not speaking, never eat or smoke during a video call. Prepare all of your materials in advance, especially if you are hosting the meeting: You don't want to keep attendants waiting while you search for a file.

Handling Diversity and Cultural Sensitivity

My three children attended a public school, and that, together with doing different extracurricular activities and family travels to different places, helped them develop an open mind and embrace diversity as a human value. However, this isn't always the case: Some young people, despite being educated and kind, spend their first 18 years in a closed environment, constrained to the same group of people with similar traits. Once they join the workforce, they may encounter some difficulties while developing cultural sensitivity.

What do we mean by diversity? It refers to a wide variety of differences between people, which includes (but isn't limited to) "race, gender, ethnic groups, age, religion, sexual orientation, citizenship status, military service, and mental and physical conditions" (Dyson, 2019). The US is demographically becoming more and more diverse, and this positively impacts the workforce. For organizations and companies, having a diverse workforce has many advantages, such as having more qualified candidates to fill key roles, gaining a wider cultural perspective to reach larger targets, and increasing both employee and customer satisfaction, to name a few.

It's up to the company to manage diversity and create policies and practices that ensure everyone feels comfortable in that work environment. However, you as an employee can also contribute by becoming aware of diversity and learning how to handle it both in your workplace and other environments as well. For example

• Accept that your colleagues come from different backgrounds than yours but treat each of them based on their individual traits, not assigning their qualities to personal bias.

• Treat each person—coworker or customer—with the same respect and follow standard rules. Applying preferential treatment weakens the morale of the staff.

• Give importance to the company's policies, inclusion-oriented seminars, and sensitivity training, which are vital for developing self-awareness, teaching them which of their actions are offensive or could be perceived as such, and how to properly communicate.

• Adopt a zero-tolerance policy when it comes to name-calling or jokes about ethnicity, gender, sexual orientation, religion, nationality, and such. This means not only should you not laugh at them, but you should also speak up if others are, and, if it happens repeatedly, report it to your superior.

Effective Communication

Communication strategies in the workplace become more important than ever. Making sure both the sender and the receiver of a message know its purpose leaves everyone satisfied, understood, and validated. But that's not all. Ineffective communication in the workplace costs *a lot* of money: According to research by Grammarly, U.S. businesses end up paying up to $1.2 trillion a year! (Jolaoso, 2023).

As it happens in handling diversity, most of the responsibility is up to company policies and your superiors. However, once you land a job, you should make an effort to improve your communication skills. This will help you reach your professional goals; generate great reports with your superiors, your colleagues, and potential customers; understand which tasks you need to prioritize; reduce potential conflict; and overall feel more engaged in your workplace.

As there are several ways of communicating, let's focus on how to improve your communication skills for each type.

Written Communication

We've already discussed some of the norms regarding email etiquette at work, such as making sure your written communication is correct, well-addressed, and you always proofread it. Each written communication must serve a specific purpose: When you write your email, consider who the receiver is, why you should communicate such a message, and get straight to the point. You use emails when you don't expect an immediate response, when you want to make a formal notification, share information and data, confirm or schedule an appointment, or notify several people at the same time.

On the other hand, you don't use emails for informal conversations, reminders, messages that need a prompt response, or sensitive topics that are much better handled in a face-to-face conversation—if you need to complain, give bad news, or provide feedback, always opt for a more personal approach.

Oral Communication

When you need to speak, make sure your tone of voice is strong and confident and avoid filler words such as "okay," "so," and "anyway," which create the impression of insecurity. You want to sound certain of what you're saying. And avoid small talk. Instead, be deliberate, plan your messages, and get straight to the point: "People are busy. Don't make them work too hard to understand what you are saying and what you need them to do" (Cooks-Campbell, 2022).

But most importantly, communicating isn't only about properly conveying your messages but also about listening to the other person. When someone at work wants to communicate with you, make sure you give them undivided attention and demonstrate it in the following ways:

• Keep eye contact and avoid distractions.

• Ask them any necessary questions to make sure the message you receive is the one they are trying to convey.

• Rephrase key aspects of their communication to demonstrate you were paying attention and you care.

• Provide positive feedback.

Nonverbal Communication

We all communicate through our body language, most of the time without realizing it. Surprisingly, more than 90% of communication is nonverbal. Albert Mehrabian, a researcher of body language, found that communication is 55% nonverbal, 38% vocal, and 7% words only (*How Much of Communication Is Nonverbal*, n.d.). Therefore, the first thing you need to do to achieve professional nonverbal communication is to be aware of how your emotions feel physically and the way you show them. You don't want to display anger, impatience, or boredom! That's why tapping your fingers, closing your fists, or rolling your eyes should be eradicated from your communications.

More than anything, your nonverbal communication should be intentional: Stand up straight, face the other person, and possibly mimic some of their gestures you find effective.

Increasing Visibility at Work

Being a responsible and accountable employee who does their tasks and manages to stay out of conflict may help you maintain your job, but it won't necessarily help you to move forward in your career. Just like those quiet students in the back of the class are less likely to be on the honor roll, slipping into the background prevents you from getting new opportunities and receiving proper recognition for your work.

Sure, you don't want to be too arrogant, bragging, or perceived as aggressive. But keeping your head down and falling into anonymity isn't the answer either: "Employee visibility essentially means getting recognition for your contribution and being included in all relevant company conversations and decisions" (Erkic, n.d.). Here are some strategies you can start implementing to increase your visibility at your workplace and make both your superiors and your colleagues notice you, give you credit for your accomplishments, and appreciate your contributions.

- **Get along with your boss:** Establish a solid rapport with your immediate superiors, as they can speak in your favor and provide you with new opportunities. Ask them for frequent feedback on how to improve your performance, and thank them for their suggestions.
- **Speak up:** Whenever you're in a meeting, don't be afraid to share your ideas or to ask questions. This may be hard if you are a shy person by nature, but it may help you to carefully read the agenda in advance and write down a few questions or contributions for when the meeting takes place. This will give you more confidence.
- **Engage in learning opportunities:** Although you may feel tempted to get up and leave whenever some event, course, seminar, or training event isn't mandatory, do the opposite and actively participate in as many as you can. They'll increase your visibility by displaying initiative, but that's not all: "Improving your skills and

qualifications can also lead to raises, promotions, and other advancement opportunities" (Castrillon, 2023).

• **Volunteer for challenging projects:** Instead of waiting for your manager to assign you a project, stand up and request them when you find out about something interesting. Besides, some projects will give you the chance to work with members of other areas to increase your exposure.

• **Give recognition and praise to others:** Highlighting your colleagues' accomplishments and giving them credit when it's due will help you maintain a humble attitude: "Sharing the credit strengthens team morale while enhancing company culture and building trust" (Castrillon, 2023).

Strategies for Increasing Visibility When Working Remotely

Work visibility can be even harder to achieve when you don't count on the proximity factor. For remote employees, raising their profile and being given adequate recognition is even more challenging: "Remote workers may feel left out of important company conversations and experience serious employee visibility problems—from fewer opportunities to meet and interact with coworkers and not feeling included in the company culture, to experiencing potential technical challenges" (Erkic, n.d.).

However, if this is your case, you mustn't give up, but adopt a visibility strategy instead. Here are some tips:

• **Always keep your camera on.** This will help people in your organization connect your name to your face, even when they rarely see you in person. Taking an active part in meetings is a must, but if they see you there, the impact is more noticeable.

• **Make sure your profile photos are up-to-date.** In the same line, if your company uses cooperative email or a messaging service, make sure your pics are clear and display the current version of you.

• **Drop by often, if possible.** Maybe you live thousands of miles away from the headquarters. But if you have the chance to regularly show your face at the office, this will remind your coworkers and superiors you're an active part of the team.

• **Work whenever everyone else is working.** An advantage of remote work is the chance to choose your schedule. But synchronicity will help you connect better with the rest of the team: "Real-time communication and collaboration will keep you in the loop with everything that's going on, and provide immediate feedback and access to shared files and information" (Erkic, n.d.).

How to Get a Promotion

Becoming more visible may help you, among other things, in getting promoted. After establishing yourself in a company where you feel comfortable and people value your skills, you'll probably be looking forward to a promotion as well. This means professional growth, more influence, more interesting tasks, and, yes, more money. But how does someone get promoted? Isn't that for the company to decide? Yes and no. On one hand, the decision to grant a promotion is for the organization to make. On the other hand, you can—and you should—act toward getting that well-deserved promotion.

How to Become Worthy of a Promotion

First of all, you need to earn that promotion by being good at your job, not just by accomplishing your regular tasks but by requesting more to showcase the different skills that the next position requires. This will prove to your superiors not only that you're great at your current position but also that you could do well taking further responsibilities and that you will fit your future position just as well. For example, a friend of mine wanted to be promoted from being a sales associate to an assistant manager. She put her focus on learning and showcasing specific managerial and other soft skills (for example, delegation and communication) instead of showcasing skills like closing sales or wider product knowledge. This highlighted her skills that fit the job she wanted, and soon, she was granted the promotion.

Keep in mind that being competent at the current level doesn't mean the same for the next level. Otherwise, you risk falling under the Peter Principle, which is an observation of a tendency in some hierarchical organizations that competent employees tend to be promoted up to the point in which they begin displaying incompetence: "As a result, according to the Peter Principle, every position in a given hierarchy will eventually be filled by employees who are incompetent to fulfill the job duties of their respective positions" (Hayes, 2023). Companies can avoid it by offering specific training both before and after the promotion takes place. In the same way, push yourself forward to develop yourself and learn the requested new skills.

Secondly, communicational skills, such as having a great rapport with others and being an active listener, also go a long way. It's okay to speak up and even to disagree sometimes, but your boss will appreciate it if they see you as a problem-solver: Instead of coming up with complaints and difficulties, make sure you also provide valuable suggestions and approaches. And be thankful when receiving constructive feedback.

Third, companies value employees who bring more value: "If you can bring in revenue (or save money), you'll be seen as a valuable part of the company. This will put you in a strong position to advocate based on your results—and justify the accompanying pay raise" (Cooks-Campbell, 2021).

How to Ask for a Promotion

Deserving a promotion is important, but it's not all. You should be proactive: If, after a while, you believe you are worthy of a promotion, you should talk about it with your boss and ask for it. Of course, this doesn't mean you'll threaten them ("Give me a promotion or I'll quit"), but instead, ask them what it will take you to be promoted. You can't expect a promotion right away, but they should offer some guidelines and a possible timelapse.

When discussing the topic, avoid comparing yourself to others: It's not "you against them." Don't bring up how another coworker got promoted while taking half of the responsibilities you are currently managing: "This can make you come across as unprofessional and criticizes both the person who was promoted and the people who agreed to promote him or her" (Petrone, 2018).

Also, keep it professional: Having a good relationship with your boss doesn't mean they ought to give you a promotion. They won't promote you because they like you but because you're right for the job. In the same way, don't turn your promotion request into a sentimental story: "You may have childcare to pay for or a sick family member, but that isn't a good reason for your company to spend more money on you. Avoid using your personal life to make the case" (Cooks-Campbell, 2021). They may care about you as a person, but what counts for getting promoted is the great work you do.

Finally, choose the right timing for the request: "Know the state of the business—along with being a key quality to getting promoted, it'll help you frame your business case" (Petrone, 2018). If the company is going through a crisis or massive layoffs, you'd better wait!

The workplace is one of the environments adults use their social skills, but it isn't the only one—and not necessarily the most important. Our following chapter will be about managing all of your relationships and establishing a good rapport with everyone around you.

Chapter 9

Social Skills—A Smart Management of Your Relationships

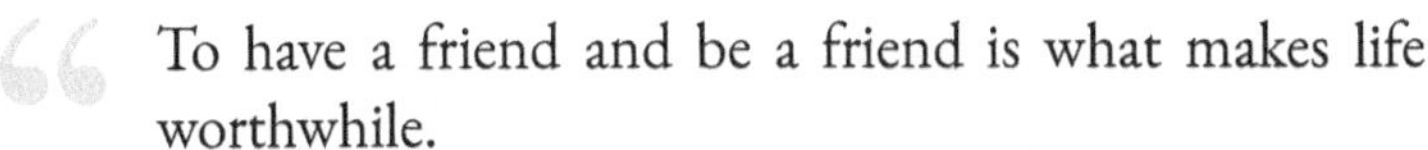

To have a friend and be a friend is what makes life worthwhile.

— Unknown, on the mutual value and fulfillment found in genuine friendships.

WHEN MY DAUGHTER Sophia was in elementary school, she kept a diary that wasn't exactly private, as she read it to the family almost every day. She wrote about her day, how she did in school, and mostly about her friends. I recall she kept a top-five list of "besties" which she updated periodically. It took almost nothing for a friend to get "banned" from the list: Maybe a classmate didn't lend her some colored pencils, or maybe she found out they didn't like the latest song by Miley Cyrus. That was it! The friend was crossed over and another friend took her place... until another event happened. It was somehow cute and annoying at the same time.

I tell you this because one trait that showed me my daughter was maturing was her new way of relating with her peers. It's not that she kept her list unchanged for longer but that she dropped such a list altogether. As she became a teen, Sophia realized that friends don't fit into categories or rankings because each human relationship is unique and precious. Now that she's 15, she has a bunch of close friends and although they may argue from time to time, that doesn't put an end to their friendship.

Becoming an adult not only means having a career and paying your car insurance, it also means learning to manage your relationships maturely. After all, human beings are social creatures by nature: We're meant to live together, so let's do it well!

Keeping in Touch With Families/Family Dynamics

Your relationship with your parents is likely to change in adolescence, and once again after you move away from your parents' home. Teenagers and young adults talk to their friends more than they do their parents. But just because you find it awkward at first, talking about everyday issues may help you reach out when you need to discuss more serious stuff, from failing an exam to finding out the person you're dating betrayed you with a friend of yours.

If you need to break some bad news to your parents, ask for their advice, or share something personal with them and you don't know where to start, try practicing putting it into words first, including how you feel: "I'm disappointed at something, and it would help me to share it with you" or "I had a problem at school, and I could really use your advice." And find a time when your parents aren't busy with something else. You can ask them if it's a good time to talk, and then find a place where you can talk quietly without interruptions. Establishing a dialogue may be difficult at first, but it will get easier with time!

Handling Family Conflict

Of course, if you had loving, supportive parents and strong family ties during your childhood, you'll find it easier to navigate through conflict and find yourself comfortable among your family members. You know by now that living with your family isn't always easy, but it helps when you feel understood and unconditionally loved.

However, most families are far from being ideal, and most

teenagers face the fact that their parents make a lot of mistakes, they don't get along with their siblings, or they need to deal with difficult situations such as a divorce, unemployment, a family loss, money worries, illnesses, and such. These unpleasant experiences may make you feel detached from your family.

However, handling conflict and going through hard times together makes it easier to navigate the storm. Talk about what's going on, maybe with one family member at a time, and take time to listen to what the other person has to say. While it's okay to take a break and spend some time alone, try to also share quality time with your family doing everyday things to strengthen your bonds. And don't forget to show appreciation for your family: They aren't perfect—neither are you—but everybody is doing the best they can.

When you were a child, you trusted your parents blindly, and by now, you understand they are flawed human beings. That doesn't make them less worthy of your love and trust, it just means you need to relate to them in a more adult way. The only exception is if you feel you are in danger. If that's the case, you shouldn't hesitate to ask for help from an adult outside your family: a teacher, a counselor, or the parent of one of your friends.

Keeping in Touch

Moving away to college is a huge step for you, and it also has an impact on your family dynamics: "You're the one dealing with an entirely new set of challenges, but your caregivers are adjusting to not having you around—and some caregivers handle that better than others" (*How to stay in touch*, n.d.). You may crave independence as your parents insist on hearing about every little detail of your life. Or, on the contrary, perhaps it's you who feels homesick and needs regular check-ups.

In any case, organizing a schedule that works both for your family and you may help you both stay connected while finding a healthy balance. Here are some suggestions for keeping in touch:

• **Start a family group chat.** If you don't have it already, now is a great moment to do it! It provides the perfect place for light exchanges, such as fun pictures, and on days when you're too busy to respond right away, you can do it later.

• **Schedule regular calls.** Of course, you can always reach out if you want to share some big news, but doing regular phone calls on specific days and times is likely to help your anxious parents, so they don't check in with you every single day. Also, if you live nearby, you can set up regular visits to your folks, especially if one of them likes to drop by unexpectedly (ugh!).

• **Keep with family traditions.** If you can't remember a single Thanksgiving without your grandmother's stuffed turkey, or Christmas doesn't feel like Christmas without snuggling under a big blanket in front of the fireplace, do your best to be with your family during the holidays. It will be easier for all of you not to see each other every day if you are still together for important rituals.

• **Use technology.** Of course, sending emails and WhatsApp messages or using FaceTime and video chat are great ways to keep in touch, even if you live thousands of miles away. But be creative! You can also play board games online with your folks and siblings, which is "a fun, low-stress way to connect with family that isn't focused on grades, how you're adjusting, or any other questions you may not always feel up for answering" (*How to stay in touch*, n.d.).

Once you move away from home, your relationship with your siblings is likely to change as well. I remember Ethan and Lucas arguing over minor things, such as choosing a TV show or having friends over. I believe, most times, their two different personalities made them crash in disagreement and conflict. But since my eldest moved away to college, the two brothers have become closer than ever; they spend a lot of time together during every visit and send each other texts, voice mails, or fun memes regularly.

Handling Friends

The social bond with peers gains importance as children approach adolescence. Teens usually spend more time talking to their friends than being with their family, and although this may be a little heartbreaking for the parents, teenage friendship is crucial for your mental health: "One study using data from more than 111,000 adolescents found that teenagers who were integrated into friendship networks had better mental health, as measured by a number of depressive symptoms" (Monroe, 2018). Teens who have solid friendships have better emotional regulation skills, a lower risk of anxiety, more empathy, and are overall happier.

Having close friends can help you deal with difficult situations you're currently going through that are normal for your age: "Friendships give adolescents and young adults a critical sense of belonging and acceptance during a tumultuous time of life. Peers are going through similar physical changes and are experiencing similar emotional struggles such as fear, insecurity, anxiety or sadness" (*Why are teen friendships so important*, 2021). There are medical studies that link close friendships with long-term resilience, which is the ability to adapt to difficult situations and emerge stronger out of them.

And your parents are right to tell you popularity isn't important for receiving these benefits: "Researchers found that people who had close friends as teens reported higher levels of self-worth and lower levels of social anxiety and depression at age 25, compared with their popular peers" (Monroe, 2018). Having thousands of followers on social media or having a large friend group with only superficial interactions won't help you thrive, having a few close friends who know you and love you the way you are will!

The Impact of Social Media on Friendships

Social media has definitely changed friendships, especially among teens and young adults. On one hand, 7 out of 10 teens claim social media helps them stay connected with their friends and even cope better with difficult times (Monroe, 2018). On the other hand, social media also has negative consequences, such as cyberbullying, feelings of being left out of social events, comparing yourself to others, or developing toxic friendships.

Social media also plays a huge role in peer pressure, way more than face-to-face interactions: "Research using brain-imaging technology shows that teens experiencing peer pressure are more likely to make risky decisions. Moreover, that's true even when the peer is anonymous and not physically present" (Monroe, 2018).

So, what conclusions can we take from the aforementioned studies? Social media can be a means of connecting with your friends, but screen time definitely shouldn't replace real-life interactions. Spending time with your friends at home, at school, in a burger joint, or at the skate park will provide you with way more benefits than simply labeling them in photos or sending them texts.

How to Build Solid Friendships?

So, having friends is so important for your happiness and mental health. Here are a few tips on how to establish and maintain strong, healthy bonds with your peers:

• **Find people you can be emotionally honest with.** A good friend will make you feel relaxed, not pressured or anxious. Reach out to those friends you feel you can truly be yourself with. Honesty means you can speak up without feeling judged, and, at the same time, they can tell you things. A true friend allows you to express your emotions and even helps you better cope with them.

• **Find people with common interests.** Joining a club, engaging in sports, arts, or any activity that you enjoy will help you make new friends who share your interests. Friendships are not about becoming twins or doing everything together. On the contrary, as you grow, you understand that you share some things with some of your friends and other things with others.

• **Create opportunities for one-on-one interactions.** We've seen how always hanging out with a huge group of people doesn't necessarily mean you have close friends. Although going to parties can be fun, try to save some time for closer social interactions: Invite one or two friends home for video games and pizza, and embrace individual talks that will give you the opportunity for deeper, meaningful social connections.

• **Trust your guts.** Conflict is a normal part of any human interaction. But if your friendship feels like it's more drama than anything else, if a so-called friend makes you always feel bad about yourself or if they pressure you into risky behaviors or behave in a manipulative way, they are not real friends. Talking to an adult about what's going on may help you put some distance and healthy boundaries between that unhealthy friendship and you.

Community Engagement and Neighbors

Back in Chapter 2, we expanded on how to appropriately deal with roommates and why you should avoid problems with your landlord and neighbors. But other than respecting the rules about quiet times and such, getting along with your neighbors can have a huge impact on your quality of life. It will give you a sense of belonging and expand your concept of home to a larger area than the little studio you rent. Here's how to be neighborly and contribute to creating a great atmosphere:

• **Study your new neighborhood or building.** Before jumping into people's lives unannounced, try to learn a little bit about your neighborhood. You can check with the landlord or simply observe. While an old lady who lives by herself may be delighted when you ring the bell to introduce yourself and hand her some flowers, the same attitude may bother the man who lives next door and is working from home.

• **Be friendly and respectful.** Introducing yourself to your neighbors and wishing them a good day whenever you see them is great, but at the same time, you don't want to act like you're suddenly their best friend. Always respect your neighbor's boundaries, and they will respect yours. This means no eavesdropping, no gossip, no asking them personal questions, and no taking sides when there's a conflict between other neighbors that don't involve you.

• **Deal with conflict face-to-face.** If you need to address an issue, such as your neighbor being loud or taking out the trash at inappropriate times, don't leave them a note or text them as you may sound too harsh: "Written complaints can seem more mean-spirited than you intended, and may shut down communication with that neighbor in the future" (Gaskill, 2013). A polite, personal talk will help your neighbor understand your point of view while, at the same time, giving them a chance to apologize or to let you know their version of the story (perhaps they weren't the ones partying all night long after all!)

• **Be respectful of common spaces.** Your apartment is crowded already, but this doesn't mean it's okay to leave your bike in the hall. A crowded common area can be dangerous—what if there was a fire?—or, at least, uncomfortable for all. And even at your place, consider that small buildings don't offer as much intimacy as a house, so anything you do inside may affect your neighbors as well: "Be aware of your drifting barbecue smoke—gas grills may be best in tight quarters. If you smoke, be respectful by not smoking where others may get secondhand smoke" (Gaskill, 2013).

Workplace Relationship Dynamics

In former chapters, we've approached how to maintain work etiquette, handle conflict, and treat everyone with respect. But your workplace may be more than just where you make a living: Strong, everlasting friendships can arise as people interact every day. We spend so much time at work that these relationships account for a big part of our human interaction, which means having solid work relationships is great for your mental well-being. On a strictly professional level, good work relationships will boost your productivity and provide you with more opportunities to grow in your career. At the same time, because you see the same people every day, you need to get along even with the ones you don't like.

Types of Work Relationships

Unlike what happens in a neighborhood or among a group of classmates, not every work relationship is symmetrical, and therefore, they are not the same. While you should treat every single person with respect and do your best to get along with all of them, some work relationships are more important than others, such as the one you maintain with your boss and your key stakeholders:

"These are the people who have a stake in your success or failure, such as customers, suppliers, and your team. Forming a bond with them will help you to ensure that your projects–and career–stay on track" (*Building good work relationships*, 2022).

Consider that team members aren't the same as coworkers: With the first ones, you need to work in collaboration to complete common projects; with the second ones, you simply work nearby. So, while being kind and polite is important in both cases, you should focus on strengthening the relationship with your team members, especially if you don't sit next to them or you don't have a lot of opportunities to interact (*10 types of workplace relationships*, 2023).

Work relationships can result in personal relationships as well. For example, a work friend is someone with whom you interact both professionally and socially: "Your work friends serve as part of your support system, and maintaining these relationships is usually mutually beneficial" (*10 types of workplace relationships*, 2023). If you see each other outside work, the relationship could end up turning into a life-long friendship. It's amazing to work with a friend, but remember that when you are at work, your interactions should remain professional out of respect for others around you.

Defining a Good Work Relationship

So, what does it mean to have a good relationship with someone you work with? These are four basic traits:

1. Mutual respect: It's the basic and first aspect of any relationship, not only at your workplace.

2. Trust: People who work together shouldn't be watching their backs.

3. Inclusion: Different opinions, insights, and traits are not only accepted but also welcomed.

4. Honest and open communication: Everyone feels free to speak up, and you've managed to effectively communicate with each other.

Some of these traits take time and effort to build and sustain, but they are all equally important.

How to Build a Solid Work Relationship

Here's what you can do to establish strong, good relationships at work:

• **Be a great professional.** As we already discussed in Chapter 8, practicing active listening, accepting feedback, and being accountable for your work will help you fulfill your duties. It will also make it easier to establish positive relationships with the people you work with.

• **Focus on giving.** See how others can benefit from your skills and strengths and become an active contributor. This will not only help you when it's you who needs support or help but also contribute to establishing a great relationship with your colleagues.

• **Retain personal details.** You don't want to come up as a stalker and comment on each Instagram post your boss publishes. But you want to remember details such as their spouse's name or follow up if they mentioned they had a sick child at home.

• **Show appreciation.** Be grateful to your colleagues, especially when they helped you accomplish a task: "Compliment them on their work, bring snacks for the break room, or send them thank-you notes. This kind of praise won't go unnoticed" (Waters, 2023).

• **Make time for catching up.** It's great to be focused on your work goals and your daily tasks, but still, schedule a regular coffee break with your coworkers to boost your relationship. This will create the time you need to build strong work relationships without neglecting your professionalism.

• **...But not too much time!** While having work friends can be fun, it's important to keep it professional all the time: "Sometimes, a work relationship can impair productivity, especially when a friend or colleague begins to monopolize your time. It's important to set your boundaries" (*Building good work relationships*, 2022).

• **...And not too close either!** Work relationships and decision-making may become compromised when you fraternize in the workplace. Fraternization is what happens when boundaries are blurred in the workplace between people who occupy different levels of authority or power, or between coworkers. It can involve romantic or overly personal relationships, or when superiors lend or borrow from subordinates. It compromises objectivity and creates discomfort for other team members, and many organizations develop policies to discourage it, or require the relationship to be declared and alerted to the HR department (Marshall, 2019).

Romantic Relationship—Building Intimacy

During your teens or early 20s, you're likely to start getting involved in romantic relationships. Maybe you've already started dating, or perhaps you still haven't found the right person—in any case, it's all right! There's no rush, and there isn't a "right time" to have a boyfriend or girlfriend. What matters the most is, if you decide to be a part of a romantic relationship, you make sure it's right both for you and the other person as well.

What Defines a Healthy Romantic Relationship?

Maybe you've already experienced that feeling of infatuation we first experience when we meet someone who rocks our world: Falling in love is something that just happens! It can feel like an adrenaline rush, our head spinning, our heart beating faster, and we become obsessed with that special person in our life.

However, falling in love and staying in love are two different things: A true relationship begins once you're no longer infatuated, but when you get to see the other person as they truly are and they see you, you both know each other's flaws, and you keep choosing each other anyway: "A healthy, secure romantic relationship can serve as an ongoing source of support and happiness in your life, through good times and bad, strengthening all aspects of your well-being" (Robinson et al., 2023). Let's see more about what a good romantic relationship looks like.

• **You both feel comfortable being yourselves.** Once you get past that infatuation stage, you get to know the other person and you accept them as they are, you aren't always trying to change your significant other despite you finding they have imperfections like any other human being—you included, of course! At the same time, you feel you don't need to play a part or fake anything when you're with them because you feel accepted for who you truly are.

• **You share an emotional connection.** Not only do you feel accepted, but you also feel valued and loved. You feel your partner is the one person who gets you. Some couples stay together because they just get along well, but this doesn't provide a stable, happy relationship in the long run.

• **You communicate openly and honestly.** The same as with your family, friends, or coworkers, you both can share your thoughts, feelings, and worries and you take the time to communicate.

• **You can respectfully disagree.** Conflict is an inherent part of any relationship, and you can argue without feeling judged or threatened: "Your partner respects your wishes and feelings and you can compromise and negotiate when there are disagreements or conflicts" (*What does a healthy relationship look like*, 2017).

• **You aren't together 24/7.** You both respect each other's space and privacy, as one relationship can't fulfill every single personal need: "Other people help make our lives satisfying but they cannot meet every need. Find what interests you and become involved. Healthy relationships have room for outside activities" (*10 tips for healthy relationships*, 2006).

• **You trust each other.** You can be vulnerable with one another because you know you can rely on the other person.

Boundaries and Consent

To feel safe in a relationship, you both need to know that the other person understands and respects their partner's boundaries. On the other hand, when one person pushes your boundaries even after knowing what they are, or if they keep crossing them, the relationship turns abusive: "Having boundaries is like drawing a line. One side has the things you are okay with and the other side, those that you are not okay with, don't feel ready for, or make you uncomfortable" (*What does a healthy relationship look like,* 2017).

For example, when my son Lucas started going out with Jackson, a boy in his class, he brought him home right away and introduced him to us. We organized a barbecue for the occasion and made sure both of them felt comfortable. Afterward, Lucas wanted to meet Jackson's parents as well. However, he wasn't okay with this as he hadn't come out to his old-fashioned dad yet. Lucas accepted it and waited until Jackson felt ready for such a big step.

A major boundary everyone needs to respect, even for brief encounters that don't qualify as relationships, is consent. It's an agreement between two people to establish that they are both freely deciding to engage in sexual activity together.

Although communication can be nonverbal (when using gestures), you need to communicate with each other to obtain consent before starting something. It must be free, voluntary, and it can be withdrawn at any time: "This means that someone can consent to one activity (kissing) but not consent to another (sex). Consent, like sex, should be about respecting each other to make their own decisions about their body" (*What does a healthy relationship look like,* 2017).

For that same reason, you can't possibly give or obtain consent if either of you is asleep, intoxicated, or not aware of what's going on. Consent can't involve force, threats, intimidation, deceit, or fraud (ACT Government Australia, 2020). It's against the law to engage in any kind of sexual activity with a person who hasn't given consent or has been coerced to do so.

Red Flags to Look For

While a healthy, happy relationship will do wonders for your well-being and the other person's, some people feel stuck in toxic relationships that can make them miserable, withdrawn from their friends and family, or even put their life in danger. Although every relationship has its ups and downs, there are some red flags that indicate things aren't working out, and you should do something about it—and, if necessary, ask for help.

• **Control.** One of you tries to change or control what the other person does (including but not limited to their clothes, their friends, or their online activity).

• **Distance.** You spend more time apart than together—maybe you even feel relieved because of that, or you keep making up excuses.

• **Imbalance.** This refers to how much each person gives in the relationship, whether emotionally, economically, or when negotiating boundaries. "Periods of inequality can happen from time to time (...) But if your relationship regularly feels unbalanced in any way, this can become problematic" (Raypole, 2019).

• **Poor communication.** One thing is handling normal relationship conflict; another thing is constantly criticizing the other person. If either of you don't feel heard, or if you talk to each other with negative language or harmful comments, you'll damage trust.

• **Fear.** More than anything, you need to feel safe around your partner. When you feel uneasy, uncomfortable, or strongly afraid to set boundaries or speak up, you may be the victim of abuse (either physical or psychological). "If you find yourself censoring everything you say because you worry about their reaction, or feel like you're 'walking on eggshells' (...), it may be time to seek professional help" (Raypole, 2019).

In this chapter, we've walked the path of building and maintaining healthy adult relationships with your family, your friends, your romantic partner, your coworkers, and your neighbors—basically, all the people around you. However, there's still one more relationship to analyze, and it's the most important of all. Our last chapter will be about your relationship with yourself and your emotional well-being.

Chapter 10

Emotional Well-Being—Because Health Goes Way Beyond Eating Whole Wheat

> Happiness is not something ready-made. It comes from your own actions.
>
> — The 14th Dalai Lama, Tenzin Gyatso, on the importance of cultivating inner peace, compassion, and positive actions as pathways to lasting emotional well-being and happiness.

BEING a teenager can be hard sometimes: Your body has experienced huge changes, and you're supposed to embrace new responsibilities but sometimes you're just not ready for them, you are discovering yourself as a person and you don't always like what you see, you realized your parents and other adults are flawed, and that the world is a challenging place to inhabit.

In the former chapters, I've given you tips on how to behave as an adult, but becoming one is also about feeling like one. That's why, in this final chapter, we'll see how to understand and manage your emotions, overcome anxiety, and turn into the best possible version of yourself as you grow up.

Mental Toughness and Resilience

You've seen it in hundreds of movies and TV series: Being a hero is not about living a quiet, peaceful, dull existence but rather about facing difficulties, falling, and finding the inner strength to get back up again and carry on after having learned from every experience. And yet, as a teenager, you sometimes feel the world collapses when you experience a drawback, such as failing an exam, having a fight with your bestie, or your parents not getting along. You may have also experienced trauma, such as losing a loved one or dealing with serious health issues.

Being an adult doesn't mean all of this will fade. We all go through difficult times! However, part of becoming an adult is acquiring mental toughness and resilience, which psychologists define "as the process of adapting well in the face of adversity, trauma, tragedy, threats, or significant sources of stress" (American Psychological Association, 2020). While there are so many aspects of life we can't control, you can learn to adapt to changes and grow from them.

Being resilient doesn't mean trauma won't affect you. You will still experience distress and emotional pain. Resilience isn't an individual personal trait you're either born with or without, but rather something that can be learned and exercised, although it takes time and effort to do so. Here's how you can foster your resilience:

• **Foster wellness.** Take care of your body (as we've seen in Chapter 1), apply daily strategies to deal with anxiety (as we'll later expand), and avoid masking your pain with alcohol or other substances.

• **Prioritize relationships**. Open up and talk to people you trust about whatever problems you are going through: "Having caring, supportive people around you acts as a protective factor during times of crisis" (Cherry, 2022b). If you are dealing with big trauma, joining a support group can help you a lot.

• **Find a life purpose.** Life's problems can discourage you. But with a sense of purpose, instead, you'll find the courage to move on from past experiences and keep going. A life purpose can be many things, such as taking part in a social movement, learning new things, serving your community, making art or music, cultivating your spirituality, or any other activities that you find meaningful.

• **Be optimistic.** Whatever you're dealing with, keep in mind circumstances are temporary, and embrace the possibility of a brighter future. And accept that most of the time, the worst possible scenarios are the ones you create in your mind. If you detect in yourself an irrational tendency to catastrophize or believe the world is out to get you, try adopting a more realistic thinking pattern (American Psychological Association, 2020).

• **Believe in yourself.** You've dealt with difficult experiences in the past, and you've managed to overcome them. Pay attention to your inner thoughts and reword the negative ones: Instead of "This is too much for me," try "This is hard, but I will learn from it." Have confidence in yourself and your abilities!

Happiness

No matter if you are a child or an adult, a teenager or an octogenarian, in the end, we all want to achieve happiness. But how do we do it? It may be easier to spot things that won't make you happy in the long run. For example, you may believe that you'll be happier once you buy the latest iPhone or brand-new designer shoes, but after spending all of your savings on them, the feeling of satisfaction and reward fades. You may also know by now that revenge, speaking ill of someone, or getting your way by losing a friendship won't help you thrive, while effectively solving conflict will.

Happiness is more profound and lasting than the immediate satisfaction of a desire or pleasure. So, what do we need to be happy? Tal Ben-Shahar, cofounder of the *Happiness Studies Academy*, defines it as "the experience of whole-person well-being," or simply "wholebeing," and adds that you can't just find happiness by pursuing it, but rather you find it after going for something else. "What could that 'something else' be? This is where the concept of 'wholebeing' comes into play, resolving the paradox by shifting our focus from the direct pursuit of happiness to the pursuit of those elements that indirectly lead to happiness" (Ben-Shahar, 2021).

Maslow's Hierarchy of Needs

Okay, we're slowly getting there. So, it turns out you don't need to look for happiness, but rather check the "happiness list" of specific elements. Back in 1943, American Psychologist Abraham Maslow published his paper *A Theory of Human Motivation* in which he developed a pyramid-shaped model that has ever since been used to describe what everyone needs to live a fulfilling, happy life (Laibowitz, n.d.). These needs are sorted into categories of different importance: You can't feel happy unless the most basic ones have been fulfilled. Let's take a closer look at Maslow's Hierarchy of Needs:

• First, there are **basic needs**, which Maslow divides into **physiological** and **safety**. You need food, water, rest, and shelter; and you need to feel safe, no matter life's unpredictability, "whether that's the safety of having a regular salary, or being free from a fatal illness, we all need some sense of security, some sense that we have 'control' over our lives" (Donovan, 2020).

• The second stage of the pyramid is the **psychological needs**. Maslow divides them into **belongingness and love** on one step and **esteem** on the following one. While the first one refers to the human need for meaningful relationships, the second one refers to a feeling of accomplishment, prestige, and being appreciated: "Whether it's through academic achievements, or sporting prowess, or professional success, it seems we both need to accomplish things, and then have those achievements recognized" (Donovan, 2020).

• Finally, on top of the pyramid, Maslow lists **self-fulfilling needs**. It's when you have all the previous needs covered and you can focus on yourself, your personal growth, and getting as close as possible to your full potential by creatively expressing yourself:

"Self-actualizing people have a grounded sense of well-being and satisfaction. And a sense of awe, wonder, and gratitude about life" (Laibowitz, n.d.)

In the following decades, Maslow expanded his model and added other levels to the top of the pyramid (namely "cognitive," "aesthetic" and, after "self-actualization," "transcendence" needs). It's worth noticing that, as it happens with any model or theory, it shouldn't be taken too literally but as a guide to reflect on how to search for a purposeful, meaningful life. Maslow's needs aren't achieved once and for good, but it's the journey that matters the most.

Self-Discipline

We've already explained the difference between dreams, plans, and goals in Chapter 5. The key to success, fulfillment, and overall happiness is learning to focus on them. By acquiring self-control, you won't waste time and energy on meaningless tasks or destructive behaviors, and you'll accomplish those goals that truly matter to you. Here's how you can increase your self-discipline:

• **Create new habits.** Practice self-discipline in your daily life so you can later apply it to specific goals. For example, get up at the same time every day (yes, even on weekends, remember your sleep routine from Chapter 1!) or include a 15-minute workout routine before you hit the shower.

• **Find a coach or a mentor.** Others can hold us accountable, but your friends and family will love you no matter what. If you need external help to move forward with your goals, pick someone who can push you ahead, even when you don't like it: "The development of expertise requires coaches who are capable of giving constructive, even painful, feedback" (Gleeson, 2020).

• **Know your weaknesses.** Like any person, you have your strengths and your flaws. So, you have a hard time getting ready for school or work? Do you hide behind your phone screen to avoid socializing? Or do you struggle to control your bad temper? Instead of pretending they don't exist and overlooking them, pay special attention to your weaknesses, as this is the only way to overcome them.

• **Get rid of temptations.** To set yourself up for success, get rid of whatever keeps interfering. Do you waste precious research time by opening new tabs on your computer and looking at memes? Then, print the articles you need to read and turn the computer off.

• **Practice self-compassion.** If you occasionally fail, this doesn't mean you are a failure. Don't give up! Forgive yourself and get back on track: "Learning how to build discipline doesn't mean tearing yourself down (...) Self-imposed threats and punishment aren't effective for developing discipline within ourselves" (Wooll, 2022).

Self-Esteem and Confidence

How is your confidence these days? What's your concept of your own person? Also known as self-regard, self-worth, or self-respect, your self-esteem includes your self-confidence, your identity, your feelings of competence and security, and a sense of belonging.

You may have a lot of people who love you, but if you don't love yourself, if you don't know and appreciate your uniqueness, you won't find inner motivation or strength to reach your personal goals. On the other hand, having overly high self-esteem may cause you relationship problems and block you from self-improvement. You need to find a balance and have healthy self-esteem (Cherry, 2022c).

People with a balanced self-esteem can
• understand their skills
• maintain healthy relationships with others
• keep realistic personal expectations
• recognize and express their needs

As teenagers, our parents may have helped us develop healthy self-esteem by loving us unconditionally, accepting failure as a path toward learning, giving praise and reassurance, listening to you, and not jumping into giving advice or solving your problems unless required. But if they fail, you can always improve your self-esteem through these strategies:

• Surround yourself with people who make you feel good about yourself. "Choose friends who help you feel OK about yourself. Find people you can be yourself with. Be that type of friend for others" (Lyness, 2018).

• Listen to that voice in your head and rephrase negative thoughts. Are you too harsh on yourself? Learn to recognize those criticisms and remarks, and turn them into something else. Don't say to yourself anything you wouldn't say to a friend.

• Focus on what's good. Do you complain a lot about your problems or your failures? Start switching the focus to your achievements or what goes well, no matter how little it seems.

• Help others. By making even a small difference in someone else's life, not only will you help them but you will also feel good about yourself.

Coping With Stress and Anxiety

We all worry from time to time. To some degree, experiencing stress is part of our daily lives. But when it becomes too frequent, it affects our mental health and well-being. After the COVID-19 pandemic, there was a worldwide increase in anxiety disorders as well as other mental health conditions, and in the US, young adults ages 18 to 25 have the highest rate of experiencing them (30.6%) (Duszynski-Goodman, 2023).

Children and younger teens also experience anxiety, which is the body's response to stress even without current stressors. This can cause physical symptoms such as digestive issues, trouble sleeping, headaches, or muscle pain and lead to more severe mental health issues. And you don't even need to experience a full traumatic event to suffer from anxiety. Sometimes, the pressure of getting accepted in college, poor self-esteem, socializing, or doing well in school can trigger anxiety. Teenagers are also affected by changes in their bodies.

At-Home Coping Strategies

If you often experience stress, you can begin by implementing basic techniques for managing your anxiety, stopping overthinking, and staying positive. How can you cope with it in your daily life?

• **Take care of your body.** Eating healthy, getting enough sleep, and exercising regularly not only keep your body fit but are also vital for improving your mental well-being. It's all part of a virtuous circle. Go back to Chapter 1 if you need to review some tips.

• **Practice meditation.** It's simple, it's free, and anyone can practice it at home. It gives you an almost immediate sense of calm and helps you ease your train of thought. There are many kinds of meditation, such as guided meditation, walking meditation, mantra meditation, Tai Chi, or yoga. The simplest exercise is closing your eyes and focusing all of your attention on breathing in and out. You can also scan your body, becoming aware of its different sensations (tension, pain, relaxation, etc.): "Combine body scanning with breathing exercises and imagine breathing heat or relaxation into and out of different parts of your body" (Mayo Clinic, 2022).

• **Mindfulness.** It's a series of techniques implemented to focus on the present time and be fully aware. Thus, you manage to turn off the volume of your worries and your thoughts about the future. By focusing on your senses and the surrounding environment, you can include these practices during your daily activities, such as when you shower, while eating, or when taking a walk outside: Notice the sounds you hear, how the air feels against your skin and hair, and whether you perceive any smell. "Keep your phone in your pocket (or better yet, at home), and do your best to stay in the moment" (Ferreira, 2020).

• **Repeat positive affirmations.** If anxiety is triggered—or triggers—negative self-talk, replace it with positive statements: "I matter," "I am enough," "This too shall pass," "I take things one day at a time," and such. You can write them down and repeat them like a mantra. It doesn't matter if you don't believe them at first: By saying them out loud, they will slowly help you reshape your negative thoughts. Several studies link the practice of positive affirmations with an activation of the brain's reward system and, therefore, reduced anxiety and stress (Casabianca & Shatzman, 2022).

How New Tech Can Help You

Thanks to new technology, you can benefit from a variety of apps designed specifically to help you improve your mental well-being. Although they won't replace professional therapy or counseling, they can help you implement relaxation techniques and better manage stress and anxiety. They prove to be useful for better implementing healthy habits, such as relaxation, getting enough sleep, or practicing mindfulness and meditation. Here are some you can try:

• **Headspace:** It offers audio meditation lessons, workout videos, and a variety of articles.

• **Calm:** It offers masterclasses, video lessons, nature scenes, and calming music.

• **iBreathe:** A free and easy-to-use app for focusing on meditation and simple breathing exercises.

• **Happify:** If you are into gamification, then you should try this app, which is based on cognitive behavioral therapy. With your weekly input, you can get a "happiness score" you can easily track to see your progress.

• **Sanvello:** It allows you to receive peer support by engaging with an online community of people with similar concerns. Those community message boards and chat groups are supervised to make sure they remain safe spaces.

Mental Health and Seeking Help

No matter how much effort and willpower you put into it, sometimes you can't deal with mental health problems on your own. This doesn't mean you are weak or not trying hard enough! On the contrary, it takes a lot of courage to admit you need help and ask for it. Begin by talking to your parents, your counselor at school, or any other adult, as they may guide you into finding professional help.

How can you tell if you need to see a therapist or start medical treatment to support your mental health? In a few words, it's when you feel your problems interfere with your daily life and you find yourself withdrawn from your friends and family or you no longer enjoy activities you used to love, your anxiety interferes with your everyday functioning, your eating or sleeping patterns change drastically, you feel utterly hopeless, or maybe when you need to find refuge in substances.

In any case, here's a list of online resources that you may find helpful:

BetterHelp: A huge network of over 30,000 online therapists. It offers convenient and affordable services worldwide. https://www.betterhelp.com/

TalkSpace: A wide variety of therapies and therapists so you can find the one kind that better suits you. https://try.talkspace.com/

Thriveworks: Another online therapy space that offers teen counseling. This one has the advantage of flexibility, so you can even find an appointment on the same day, and it offers a lenient cancellation policy. https://thriveworks.com/

Open Path Collective: If you don't have health insurance and you worry you won't be able to afford a therapist, this website connects you with pre-licensed therapists who can offer you affordable care. https://openpathcollective.org/

The Trevor Project: A safe space for LGBTQ young people where you can find trained crisis counselors who will reach out for free. https://www.thetrevorproject.org/crisis-services/

988 Suicide & Crisis Lifeline: If you or one of your friends is having suicidal thoughts, don't hesitate to reach out for immediate help. You can either call, text, or chat 988 (formerly 1-800-273-8255). https://988lifeline.org/current-events/the-lifeline-and-988/

This is the last chapter of the book because I am convinced that it's the most important of them all. Being an adult is, more than anything, being a person who actively lives the life they create and not just a bystander of life's events.

Understanding how you can search for everything you need to

be happy, build your self-confidence, believe in yourself, become resilient when you deal with the unexpected, and ask for help when you can't handle all on your own will help you when dealing with all of the other topics we covered in previous chapters. Being comfortable being you, in the end, is the key to thriving as a young adult and heading toward a long, productive, and exciting life!

Conclusion

We've come to the end of the book, but your adult life is just beginning. Sculpting yourself from being a teen into a successful adult is not something to achieve in a couple of days but a long, delicate process, especially since you are, at the same time, the artist and the work of art. Hopefully, after reading this book, you'll feel confident you have the right tools but more, that you are made from the most beautiful piece of marble, and you deserve to shine.

After learning about common adult duties such as household tasks, driving, managing money, or starting a career, don't try to attempt it all at once. The first step is for you to raise self-awareness to identify your strengths and weaknesses and, therefore, the areas you need to work most to improve. As you get to know yourself better, you'll build inner strength, grit, confidence, and resilience.

By improving your communication skills, not only will you smartly manage all of your relationships, but you'll also enable internal speech and external expression and framing of thoughts. In the end, this will develop creative skills and resourcefulness, finally aided by critical thinking to ultimately become an independent, self-thinking adult not easily influenced by life circumstances.

I don't want to say goodbye without thanking you for reading this book. Hopefully, by now, you feel more prepared to enter adulthood with a positive mindset. One last favor: If you enjoyed reading it, please leave a review so other teens and young adults can benefit from it as you did.

As a parent, I try to do my best to guide my children into a happy, fulfilling adulthood. Ethan enjoys his career while keeping a healthy work-life balance. Recently, he got engaged, and he plans to start his own family shortly. Lucas is finishing high school and looks forward to launching his own company. And Sophia, still in her teens, has surrounded herself with a great group of friends who encourage her dream to go to college and maybe take a year to travel the world.

These are my children's dreams and goals.

Now find yours and go achieve them!

Chapter "Good Will"

Helping others without expectation of anything in return has been proven to lead to increased happiness and satisfaction in life.

I would love to give you the chance to experience that same feeling during your reading experience today...

All it takes is a few moments of your time to answer one simple question:

<u>Would you make a difference in the life of someone you've never met—without spending any money or seeking recognition for your good will?</u>

If so, I have a small request for you.

If you've found value in your reading experience today, I humbly ask that you take a brief moment right now to leave an honest review of this book. It won't cost you anything but 30 seconds of your time—just a few seconds to share your thoughts with others.

Your voice can go a long way in helping someone else find the same inspiration and knowledge that you have!

<u>Leave a review on Amazon</u>

☆☆☆☆☆

References

ACT Government Australia. (2020). *Developing personal safety skills for young people.* ACT Education. https://www.education.act.gov.au/__data/assets/pdf_-file/0005/2077196/Developing-Personal-Safety-Skills-for-Young-People.pdf

Allen, D. (2015). *Getting things done: The art of stress-free productivity.* Penguin Books.

American Academy of Pediatrics. (2016, March 1). *A teenager's nutritional needs.* Healthy Children. https://www.healthychildren.org/English/ages-stages/teen/nutrition/Pages/A-Teenagers-Nutritional-Needs.aspx

American Psychological Association. (2020, February 1). *Building your resilience.* https://www.apa.org/topics/resilience/building-your-resilience

Annisa, S. (2021, June 13). *Ikigai: Find your passion, mission, vocation, and profession.* Medium. https://safiraans.medium.com/ikigai-find-your-passion-mission-vocation-and-profession-6e1299ad80f2

Axelton, K. (2020, March 25). *10 things first-time car buyers need to know.* Experian. https://www.experian.com/blogs/ask-experian/tips-for-first-time-car-buyers/

Barnes, M. (2021, October). *Talking to your parents or other adults.* Kids Health. https://kidshealth.org/en/teens/talk-to-parents.html

Basic car maintenance tips & services checklist. (n.d.) Toyota. https://www.toyota.com/car-tips/basic-car-maintenance-tips-services-checklist.

Basic foods checklist: How to stock your kitchen for simple meals. (2020). UNL Food. https://food.unl.edu/article/basic-foods-checklist-how-stock-your-kitchen-simple-meals

Benson, F. (2022, November 28). *What happens to your digital footprint when you die?* IFL Science. https://www.iflscience.com/what-happens-to-your-digital-footprint-when-you-die-66262

Ben-Shahar, T. (2021, November 21). *The five things you need to be happy, according to a happiness expert.* BBC Science Focus. https://www.sciencefocus.com/the-human-body/five-things-to-be-happy

Birt, J. (2022, September 30). *Top organizational skills: Examples and how to develop them.* Indeed. https://www.indeed.com/career-advice/career-development/organizational-skills

Bizga, A. (2023, March 15). *The digital you in 2023: Modern digital footprints and their impact on privacy and security.* Bitdefender. https://www.bitdefender.com/blog/hotforsecurity/the-digital-you-in-2023-modern-digital-footprints-and-their-impact-on-privacy-and-security/

Blanton, K. (2022, March 28). *10 meal prep tips every beginner should know.* Everyday Health. https://www.everydayhealth.com/diet-nutrition/meal-prep-tips-every-beginner-should-know/

References

Borsellino, R. (2021, March 3). *The 31 best LinkedIn profile tips for job seekers*. The Muse. https://www.themuse.com/advice/linkedin-profile-tips

Brown, M. (2019). *Personal safety for young adults*. Sutter Health. https://www.sutter-health.org/health/young-adults/adulting/personal-safety

Brown, T. & Kho, E. (2023, May 10). *How to rent an apartment [2023 rental application guide]*. Apartment List. https://www.apartmentlist.com/renter-life/rental-apartment-application-process

Browning, C. (2021, December 9). *A money expert says this is the 'perfect number of bank accounts to have—here's how she sets it up*. CNBC. https://www.cnbc.com/2021/12/09/the-perfect-number-of-bank-accounts-you-need-to-save-money-according-to-money-expert.html

Building good work relationships. (2022). Mind Tools. https://www.mindtools.com/aorqe4z/building-good-work-relationships

Caramela, S. (2023, August 4). *Tips for creating a great resume*. Business News Daily. https://www.businessnewsdaily.com/3207-resume-writing-tips.html

Car maintenance basics everyone should know. (2023, May 26). Family Handyman. https://www.familyhandyman.com/list/car-maintenance-basics-everyone-should-know/

Casabianca, S. & Shatzman, C. (2022, April 25). *46 positive affirmations for anxiety relief*. PsychCentral. https://psychcentral.com/anxiety/affirmations-for-anxiety

Castrillon, C. (2023, March 19). *5 ways to increase your visibility at work*. Forbes. https://www.forbes.com/sites/carolinecastrillon/2023/03/19/5-ways-to-increase-your-visibility-at-work/?sh=5eb9d6132f2d

Chen, M. (2022, July 28). *Zoom meeting etiquettes for everyone | Updated 2023*. Notta. https://www.notta.ai/en/blog/zoom-meeting-etiquette

Cherry, K. (2022a, November 14). *What is procrastination?* Very Well Mind. https://www.verywellmind.com/the-psychology-of-procrastination-2795944

Cherry, K. (2022b, October 6). *10 ways to build resilience*. Very Well Mind. https://www.verywellmind.com/ways-to-become-more-resilient-2795063

Cherry, K. (2022c, November 7). *What is self-esteem?* Very Well Mind. https://www.verywellmind.com/what-is-self-esteem-2795868

Cleaning basics. (n.d.). Cleaning Institute. https://www.cleaninginstitute.org/cleaning-tips/clean-home/cleaning-basics. Retrieved on 2023, August 23.

Cooks-Campbell, A. (2022, July 14). *Communication is key in the workplace. Here's how to improve*. BetterUp. https://www.betterup.com/blog/why-communication-is-key-to-workplace-and-how-to-improve-skills

Cooks-Campbell, A. (2021, June 17). *How to get promoted, the do's and don'ts*. BetterUp. https://www.betterup.com/blog/how-to-get-promoted

Could you live without a car? (2018, September 6). Capital One. https://www.capitalone.com/bank/money-management/life-events/living-without-a-car/

Davies, S.T. (2023, August 15). *How to set up GTD in Notion (the only guide you need)*. Samuel Thomas Davies. https://www.samuelthomasdavies.com/how-to-set-up-gtd-in-notion/

Devine, M. (2020). *How to create a culture of accountability in your home*. Empowering

References

Parents. https://www.empoweringparents.com/article/how-to-create-a-culture-of-accountability-in-your-home/

Donovan, C. (2020, December 6). *The 5 basic "needs" we all need to be happy*. Elephant Journal. https://www.elephantjournal.com/2020/12/maslows-hierarchy-of-needs-a-happiness-shopping-list/

Dorm VS. apartment. What's right for you? (2022). The Scholarship System. https://thescholarshipsystem.com/blog-for-students-families/dorm-vs-apartment-whats-right-for-you/

Driver's license in the USA. (n.d.). The American Dream. https://www.the-american-dream.com/drivers-license-usa/ Retrieved on 2023, August 24.

Driving age by state 2022/2023. (2023). Population U. https://www.populationu.com/gen/driving-age-by-state

Duszynski-Goodman, L. (2023, September 4). *Mental health statistics*. Forbes. https://www.forbes.com/health/mind/mental-health-statistics/

Dyson, E. (2019). *Managing diversity in the workplace*. People Scout. https://www.peoplescout.com/insights/managing-diversity-in-workplace/

Effective scheduling. (n.d.). Mind Tools. https://www.mindtools.com/ak2ljl6/effective-scheduling. Retrieved on 2023, August 31.

Erkic, A. (n.d.). *How to increase visibility at work as a remote worker*. Puble. https://pumble.com/blog/increase-visibility-at-work-as-a-remote-worker/. Retrieved on 2023, September 8.

Marshall, D. (2019, September 17). *Examples of Fraternization in the Workplace*. The Nest. https://woman.thenest.com/power-relationships-between-men-women-workplace-19917.html.

An essential guide for building an emergency fund. (n.d.). Consumer Financial Protection Bureau. https://www.consumerfinance.gov/an-essential-guide-to-building-an-emergency-fund/. Retrieved on 2023, August 30.

Ferreira, M. (2020, February 11). *14 mindfulness tricks to reduce anxiety*. Healthline. https://www.healthline.com/health/mindfulness-tricks-to-reduce-anxiety

57 smart questions to ask in a job interview in 2023. (2023, March 3). The Muse. https://www.themuse.com/advice/51-interview-questions-you-should-be-asking

5 perks of living in an apartment vs. a college dorm. (2021, August 18). Student Room Stay. https://blog.studentroomstay.com/5-perks-of-living-in-an-apartment-vs-a-college-dorm

Gaskill, L. (2013, August 19). *How to get along with the neighbors—and live happier at home*. Houzz. https://www.houzz.com/magazine/how-to-get-along-with-the-neighbors-and-live-happier-at-home-stsetivw-vs~16058633

Getting along with family. (2019). Kids Helpline. https://kidshelpline.com.au/teens/issues/getting-along-family

Gleeson, B. (2020, August 25). *9 powerful ways to cultivate extreme self-discipline*. Forbes. https://www.forbes.com/sites/brentgleeson/2020/08/25/8-powerful-ways-to-cultivate-extreme-self-discipline

Gold, B. (2022, July 15). *8 easy tips to make your weekly meal prep a breeze*. Real Simple. https://www.realsimple.com/food-recipes/cooking-tips-techniques/meal-prep-tips

Gorton, D. (2023, March 31). *Taxes definition: Types, who pays, and why.* Investopedia. https://www.investopedia.com/terms/t/taxes.asp

Gregory, L. (2022, March 21). *13 items you absolutely must include in a roommate agreement.* Apartment Guide. https://www.apartmentguide.com/blog/roommate-agreement-essential-topics/

Haagensen, E. (2023, March 2). *Finance terms for beginners.* Investopedia. https://www.investopedia.com/articles/investing/061313/10-common-financial-terms-every-newbie-needs-know.asp

Half, R. (2016). *How to prepare for a job interview.* Robert Half. https://www.roberthalf.com.au/career-advice/interview

Hanson, M. (2023, June 25). *Average cost of college & tuition.* Education Data Initiative. https://educationdata.org/average-cost-of-college

Hayes, A. (2023, August 30). *The Peter Principle: What it is and how to overcome it.* Investopedia. https://www.investopedia.com/terms/p/peter-principle.asp

Helhoski, A. (2021, August 10). *6 things to know about student loans before you start school.* Nerd Wallet. https://www.nerdwallet.com/article/loans/student-loans/6-things-to-know-about-student-loans-before-freshman-year

Home maintenance checklist: 10 easy things to do monthly. (n.d.). Travelers. https://www.travelers.com/resources/home/maintenance/home-maintenance-checklist-10-easy-things-to-do-monthly. Retrieved on 2023, August 23.

How much deep, light, and REM sleep do you need? (2023, February 17). Texas Health. https://www.texashealth.org/areyouawellbeing/Health-and-Well-Being/How-Much-Deep-Light-and-REM-Sleep-Do-You-Need

How much of communication is nonverbal? (n.d.). The University of Texas Permian Basin. https://online.utpb.edu/about-us/articles/communication/how-much-of-communication-is-nonverbal/. Retrieved on 2023, October 7.

How to choose a career: 7 ways to narrow your options. (2023, June 15). Coursera. https://www.coursera.org/articles/how-to-choose-a-career

How to dress for work: 4 types of office dress codes. (2021, June 7). MasterClass. https://www.masterclass.com/articles/how-to-dress-for-work

How to dress professional: What it is and why it's important. (2021, June 29). Glassdoor. https://www.glassdoor.com/blog/guide/how-to-dress-professional/

How to get promoted at work: 9 effective strategies. (2023, February 3). Indeed. https://www.indeed.com/career-advice/career-development/how-to-get-promoted-at-work

How to make a budget: Your step-by-step guide. (2023, August 24). Ramsey Solutions. https://www.ramseysolutions.com/budgeting/how-to-make-a-budget

How to make decisions. (n.d.). Mind Tools. https://www.mindtools.com/aiplsat/how-to-make-decisions. Retrieved on 2023, September 4.

How to stay in touch with your family in college. (n.d.). The Jed Foundation. https://jed-foundation.org/resource/how-to-stay-in-touch-with-your-family-in-college/. Retrieved on 2023, September 11.

Hutchinson, D. (2023, June 20). *Michigan parents describe night of son's suicide, dangers of sextortion, how he was targeted*. Click on Detroit. https://www.clickon-detroit.com/news/local/2023/06/20/michigan-parents-describe-night-of-sons-suicide-dangers-of-sextortion-how-he-was-targeted/

The importance of dressing professionally at work. (2023, March 10). Indeed. https://www.indeed.com/career-advice/starting-new-job/importance-dressing-professionally-at-work

Increasing your visibility. (n.d.). Mind Tools. https://www.mindtools.com/arnm-lep/increasing-your-visibility. Retrieved on 2023, September 8.

Ingram, J. (2022, November 7). *How to choose a career: 8 ways to make the decision*. U.S. News. https://money.usnews.com/careers/articles/how-to-choose-a-career

Itani, O. (2021, March 12). *How living by your personal values helps you become more intentional in your life decisions*. Omar Itani. https://www.omaritani.com/blog/personal-values-and-intentional-living

James. (2022). *Zoom etiquette: 15 do's and don'ts for any Zoom meeting*. Social Intents. https://www.socialintents.com/blog/zoom-etiquette-15-zoom-meeting-rules-everyone-should-follow/

Jarvie, M. (2016, November 2). *Storing potatoes for quality and food safety*. Michigan State University Extension. https://www.canr.msu.edu/news/storing_potatoes_for_quality_and_food_safety

Jolaoso, C. (2023, May 10). *10 tips for effective communication in the workplace*. Forbes. https://www.forbes.com/advisor/business/effective-communication-workplace/

Kaspersky. (2021). *What is a digital footprint? And how to protect it from hackers*. Kaspersky. https://www.kaspersky.com/resource-center/definitions/what-is-a-digital-footprint

Keiling, H. (2023, August 31). *How to prepare for an interview in 11 steps*. Indeed. https://www.indeed.com/career-advice/interviewing/how-to-prepare-for-an-interview

Kelly, A. (2019, January 16). *Take charge of your health: A guide for teenagers*. National Institute of Diabetes and Digestive and Kidney Diseases. https://www.niddk.nih.gov/health-information/weight-management/take-charge-health-guide-teenagers

Kubala, J. (2022, June 20). *Healthy eating for teens: A complete guide*. Healthline. https://www.healthline.com/nutrition/healthy-eating-for-teens

Laibowitz, A. (n.d.) *Maslow's Hierarchy of Needs: The pyramid of happiness*. Happiness.com. https://www.happiness.com/magazine/science-psychology/what-is-maslows-pyramid/ Retrieved on 2023, September 13.

Landry, L. (2018, October 11). *Financial terminology: 20 financial terms to know*. Harvard Business School Online. https://online.hbs.edu/blog/post/finance-for-non-finance-professionals-finance-terms-to-know

Ley, S. & Hutchinson, D. (2023, August 19). *Nigerian men charged in sextortion case that caused 17-year-old Michigan boy to die by suicide*. Click on Detroit. https://www.clickondetroit.com/news/michigan/2023/08/19/nigerian-men-charged-in-sextortion-case-that-caused-17-year-old-michigan-boy-to-die-by-suicide/

Llobe. (2021, February 18). *10 reasons why home-cooked food is better than takeout*.

Vaya. https://vaya.in/10-reasons-why-home-cooked-food-is-better-than-takeout/

Low, K. (2023, August 30). *12 ways to deal with chronic procrastination*. Very Well Mind. https://www.verywellmind.com/overcoming-chronic-procrastination-20390

Lyness, D. (2022). *How can I improve my self-esteem?* Kids' Health. https://kidshealth.org/en/teens/self-esteem.html

Markovitz, N. (2022, October 16). *Even in your 20s, you should have a doctor you can see regularly*. The Washington Post. https://www.washingtonpost.com/wellness/2022/10/16/20-somethings-doctor-visits/

Maurice, K. (2017). *7 steps to turn your dreams into goals and achieve them*. Tools Hero. https://www.toolshero.com/personal-development/7-steps-turn-dreams-goals-achieve/

Mayo Clinic. (2022, April 29). *Meditation: A simple, fast way to reduce stress*. https://www.mayoclinic.org/tests-procedures/meditation/in-depth/meditation/art-20045858

McCallum, M. (2016, July 18). *The most dangerous quote if you "do what you love for a living."* LinkedIn. https://www.linkedin.com/pulse/most-dangerous-quote-you-do-what-love-living-marlene-mccallum/

McKay, D. R. (2022, September 13). *How To make a career choice when you are undecided*. The Balance. https://www.thebalancemoney.com/steps-to-choosing-career-525506

Miles, M. (2022, May 12). *4 ways to overcome your quarter-life crisis (and redefining success)*. Better Up. https://www.betterup.com/blog/quarter-life-crisis

Mishra, A. (2023, February 10). *Workplace etiquette: Tips for beginners and professionals*. LinkedIn. https://www.linkedin.com/pulse/workplace-etiquette-tips-beginners-professionals-alakshendra-mishra/

Monroe, J. (2018). *The importance of teen friendships*. Newport Academy. https://www.newportacademy.com/resources/empowering-teens/teen-friendships/

Moran, J. (2022). *The 6 types of procrastinator and how they think*. Jayson Moran. https://jaysonmoran.com/behaviour-change/the-6-types-of-procrastinator-and-how-they-think/

Northup, G. (2023, August 31). *10 resume writing tips to help you land a position*. Indeed. https://www.indeed.com/career-advice/resumes-cover-letters/10-resume-writing-tips

Oh, H. (2022, August 11). *13 ways for teenagers to save money with (or without) a job*. Seventeen. https://www.seventeen.com/life/school/a40670024/how-to-save-money-teenager/

Oliver, V. (2021, November 11). *10 common job interview questions and how to answer them*. Harvard Business Review. https://hbr.org/2021/11/10-common-job-interview-questions-and-how-to-answer-them

Owens, H. & Shea, A. (2023, June 22). *The 13 best online therapy services that are tried, tested, and expert-approved*. Very Well Mind. https://www.verywellmind.com/best-online-therapy-4691206

Palmquist, K. (2023, July 6). *13 essential tips to follow for proper etiquette at work.* Indeed. https://www.indeed.com/career-advice/career-development/etiquette-at-work

Petrone, P. (2018, October 1). *How to get promoted—The complete guide to moving up.* LinkedIn. https://www.linkedin.com/business/learning/blog/productivity-tips/how-to-get-promoted

Pinola, M. & Tepper, T. (2023, July 25). *The best budgeting apps.* The New York Times. https://www.nytimes.com/wirecutter/reviews/best-budgeting-apps-and-tools

Pirulis, A. (2019, January 18). *How to rent your first apartment.* Apartments.com. https://www.apartments.com/blog/how-to-rent-your-first-apartment

Raypole, C. (2019, December 13). *What makes a relationship healthy?* Healthline. https://www.healthline.com/health/healthy-relationship

Regan, S. (2022, February 17). *Are you going through a quarter-life crisis? What experts want you to know.* Mind Body Green. https://www.mindbodygreen.com/articles/quarter-life-crisis

Riserbato, R. (2022, September 14). *15+ organizational skills every leader needs [+ ways to develop them].* Hubspot. https://blog.hubspot.com/marketing/organizational-skills

Robinson, L., Smith, M. & Segal, J. (2023, February 28). *Tips for building a healthy relationship.* Help Guide. https://www.helpguide.org/articles/relationships-communication/relationship-help.htm

Santillan, M. (2020, July 19). *The Millennial question: Are the 30s the new 20s?* Marron Is Going. https://marronisgoing.com/the-millennial-question-are-the-30s-the-new-20s/

Schwartz, N. (2022, September 27). *15 tips to build self-esteem and confidence in teens.* Big Life Journal. https://biglifejournal.com/blogs/blog/build-self-esteem-confidence-teens

Scholarships: all you need to know. (n.d.). Study Portals. https://www.scholarshipportal.com/article/scholarships-all-you-need-to-know. Retrieved on 2023, August 29.

Sergeeva, I. (2021, March 11). *Accountability vs. responsibility for leaders: back to the basics.* Better Up. https://www.betterup.com/blog/accountability-vs-responsibility-for-leaders-going-back-to-the-basics

7 ways to help your teen strengthen their friendships. (n.d.). Reach Out Parents. https://parents.au.reachout.com/common-concerns/everyday-issues/things-to-try-peer-pressure/help-your-teenager-make-great-friends. Retrieved on 2023, September 11.

Sharma, S. (2023, February 22). *7 steps of goal-setting: How to achieve your dreams.* Risely. https://www.risely.me/steps-of-goal-setting-how-to-achieve-your-dreams/

Shatz, I. (n.d.). *Procrastination types: Understanding the different ways people procrastinate.* Solving Procrastination. https://solvingprocrastination.com/procrastination-types/. Retrieved on 2023, September 4.

Sippl, A. (2020). *7 organizational skills to teach your teen.* Life Skills Advocate. https://lifeskillsadvocate.com/blog/7-organization-skills-to-teach-your-teen/

References

Smith, J. (2015, April 28). *19 business etiquette rules every professional should know.* World Economic Forum. https://www.weforum.org/agenda/2015/04/19-business-etiquette-rules-every-professional-should-know/

Smith, S. (2016, April 29). *6 weird facts about your body.* Texas A&M University. https://vitalrecord.tamhsc.edu/6-weird-body-facts/

Stetka, B. (2017, September 19). *Extended adolescence: When 25 is the new 18.* Scientific American. https://www.scientificamerican.com/article/extended-adolescence-when-25-is-the-new-181/

Suder, R. (2016). *How to use LinkedIn to get a job.* Top Resume. https://www.topresume.com/career-advice/14-ways-to-leverage-your-linkedin-profile-during-your-job-search

Teens and stress: When it's more than worry. (2023, May 18). NIH Medline Plus. https://magazine.medlineplus.gov/article/teens-and-stress-when-its-more-than-worry

10 benefits of effective communication in the workplace. (2023, February 23). Indeed. https://www.indeed.com/career-advice/career-development/communication-benefits

10 tips before buying your first car. (2020, April 17). Bingle. https://www.bingle.com.au/hub/owning-a-car/buying-your-first-car.html

10 tips for healthy relationships. (2006). Amherst College. https://www.amherst.edu/campuslife/health-safety-wellness/counseling/self_care/healthy_relationships/10_tips_for_health_relationships

10 types of workplace relationships and how to improve them. (2023, March 10). Indeed. https://www.indeed.com/career-advice/career-development/types-of-workplace-relationships

USAA. (2023, July 12). *10 tips for buying your first car.* https://www.usaa.com/inet/wc/advice-finances-buying-your-first-car?akredirect=true

US Department of Agriculture and US Department of Health and Human Services. (2020, December). Dietary Guidelines for Americans, 2020-2025. 9th Edition. https://www.dietaryguidelines.gov/sites/default/files/2020-12/Dietary_Guidelines_for_Americans_2020-2025.pdf#page=31

Valladolid, B. (2021, September 22). *Effective leadership: The difference between responsibility and accountability.* Gingr Tech. https://gingr.tech/blog/effective-leadership-difference-between-responsibility-and-accountability/

Walker, M. (2018). *Why we sleep: Unlocking the power of sleep and dreams.* Penguin Books.

Waters, S. (2023, February 8). *Why building great work relationships is more than just getting along.* Better Up. https://www.betterup.com/blog/building-good-work-relationships

Wei, J. (2022, September 19). *Insurance 101: A guide for parents and teens.* My Doh. https://www.mydoh.ca/learn/money-101/insurance/insurance-101-a-guide-for-parents-and-teens/

Weliver, D. (2023, August 18). *Budgeting for teens: Grow your money while you're young*. Money Under 30. https://www.moneyunder30.com/budgeting-for-teens/

Weng, W.S. (2023, February 28). *Doc Talk: The link between sleeping too little, or too much, and cancer*. The Straits Time. https://www.straitstimes.com/life/doc-talk-the-link-between-sleeping-too-little-or-too-much-and-*cancer*

What does a healthy relationship look like? (2017). New York State. https://www.ny.gov/teen-dating-violence-awareness-and-prevention/what-does-healthy-relationship-look

What is a digital footprint? (n.d.) Malware Bytes. https://www.malwarebytes.com/cybersecurity/basics/digital-footprint. Retrieved on 2023, September 5.

What is GDT? (2019). Getting Things Done. https://gettingthingsdone.com/what-is-gtd/

What should I wear? The ultimate guide to workplace dress codes. (2023, June 2). The Washington Center. https://resources.twc.edu/articles/what-should-i-wear-to-work

Why are teen friendships so important to mental health? (2021, February 25). Thrive. https://www.thrivetrainingconsulting.com/why-are-teen-friendships-so-important-to-mental-health/

Wigmore, I. (2017). *Definition: Adulting*. What Is.com. https://www.techtarget.com/whatis/definition/adulting

Wooll, M. (2022, February 24). *Developing the discipline of self-discipline*. Better Up. https://www.betterup.com/blog/how-to-be-disciplined

York, A. (2023, January 27). *12 best free schedule makers to improve productivity*. ClickUp. https://clickup.com/blog/best-free-schedule-maker/